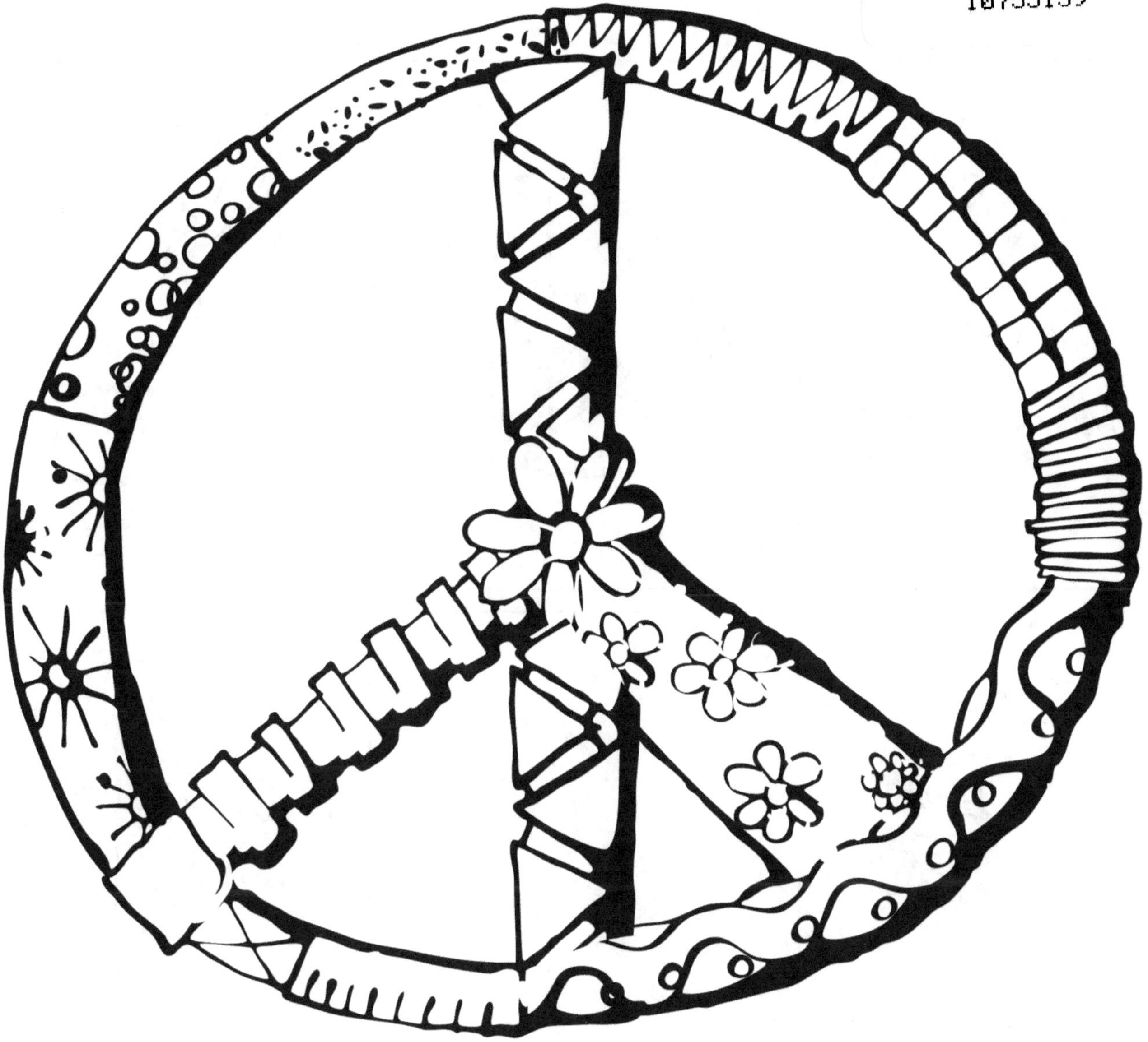

Coloring Book For Teens

Anti-Stress Designs Vol 7

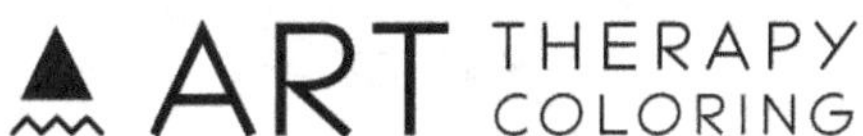

Preview of Coloring Pages

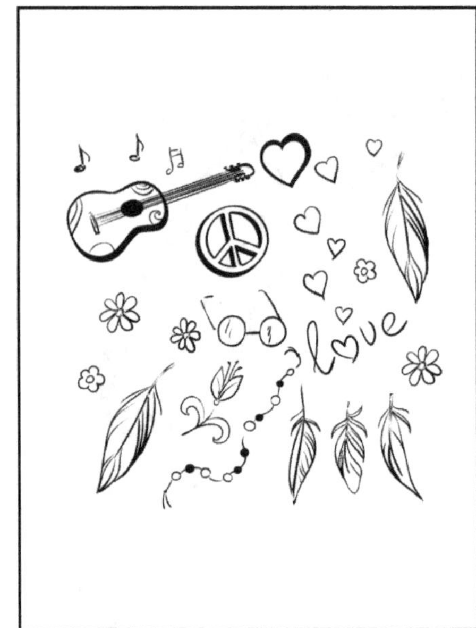

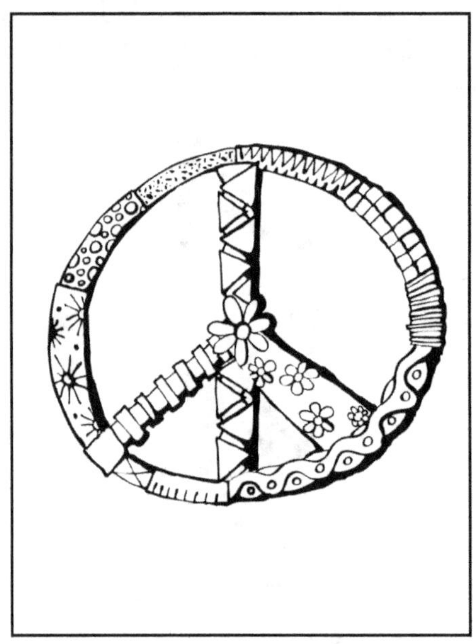

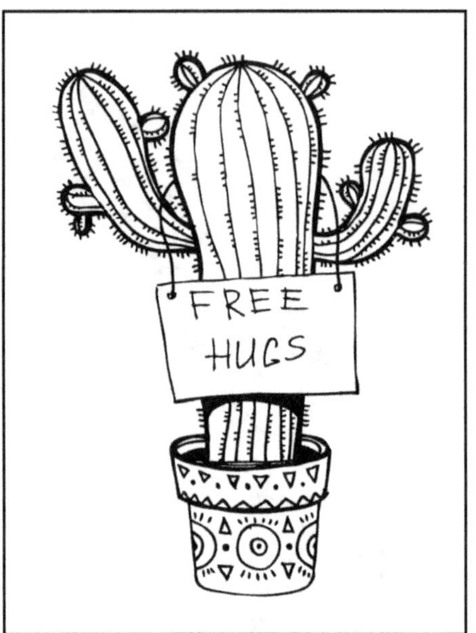

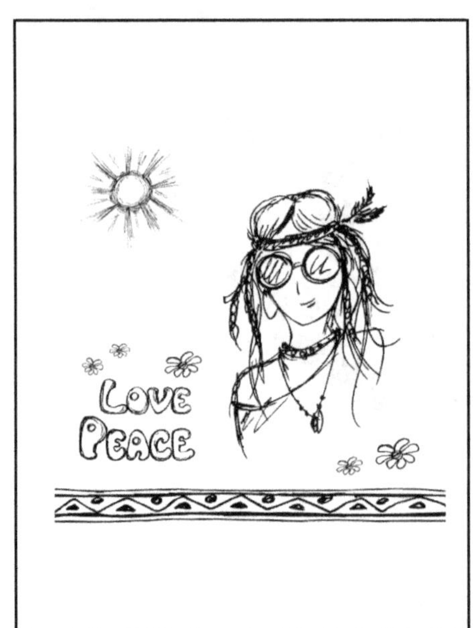

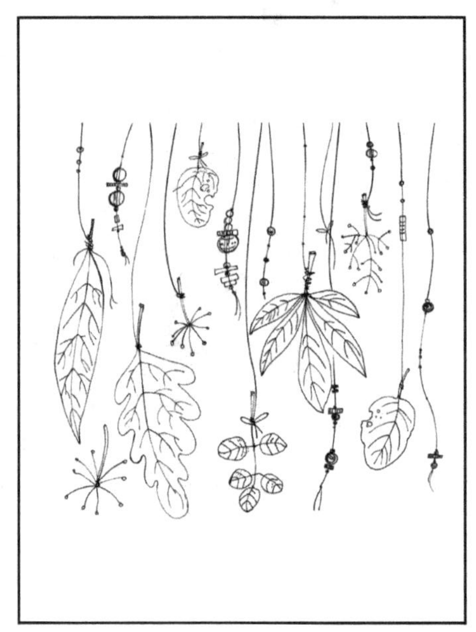

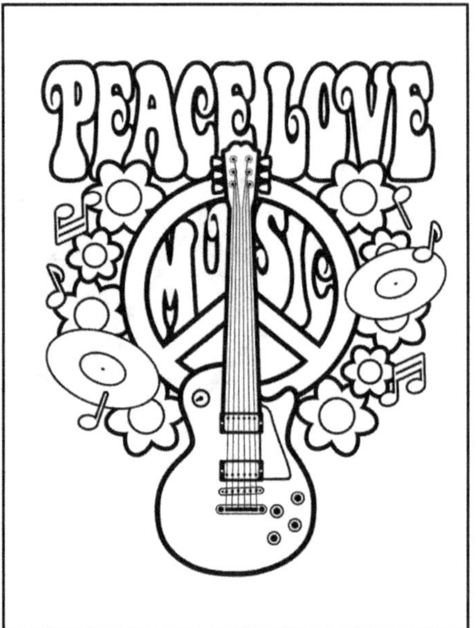

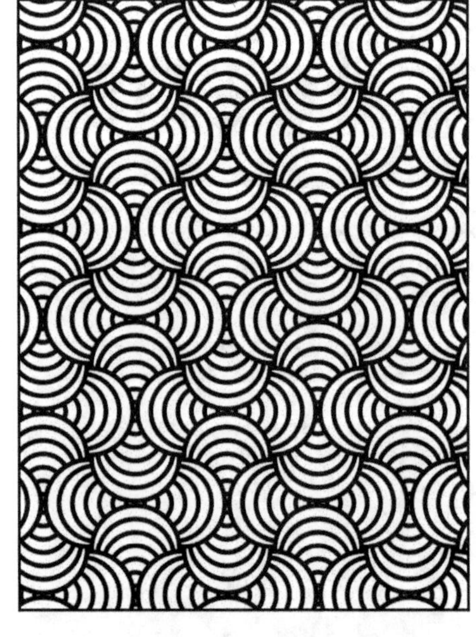

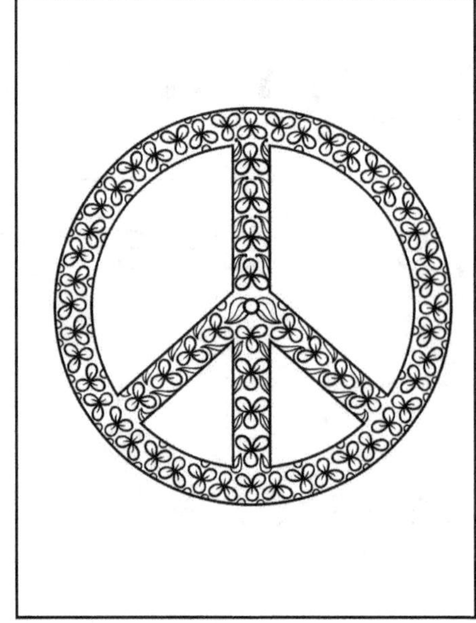

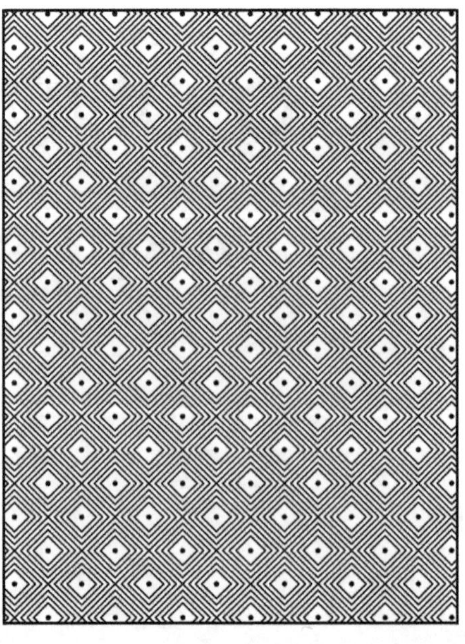

www.arttherapycoloring.com

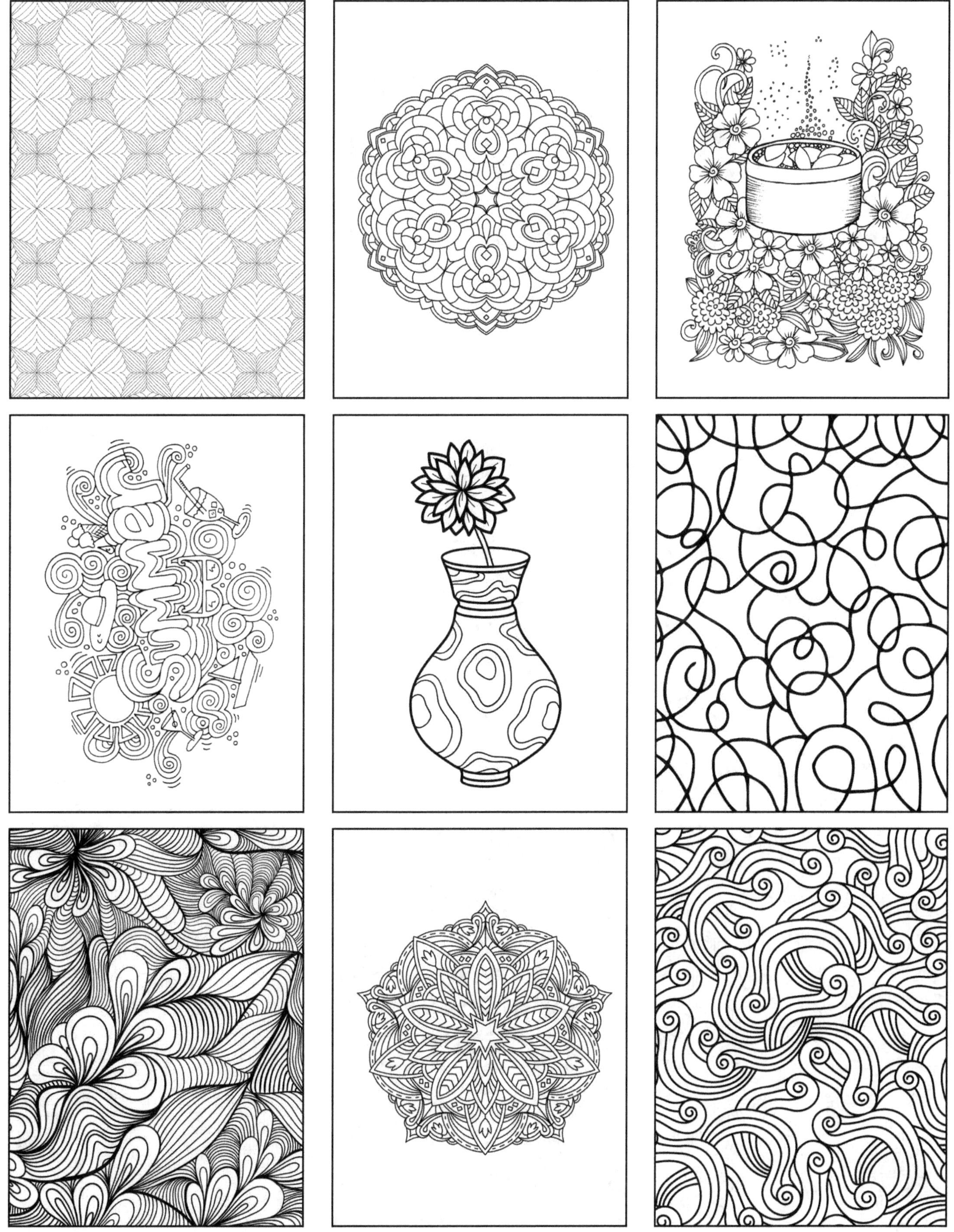

Preview of Coloring Pages

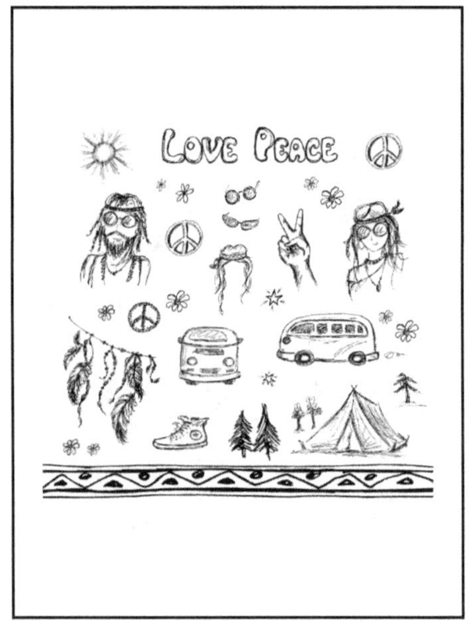

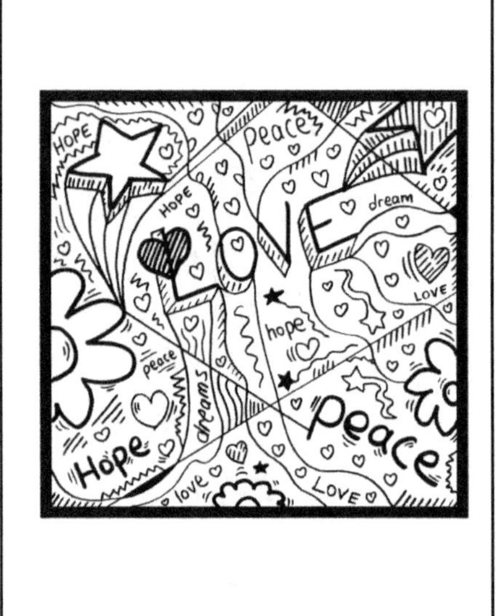

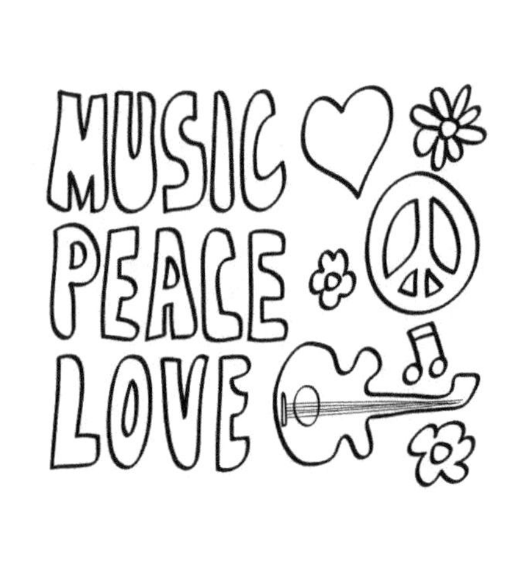

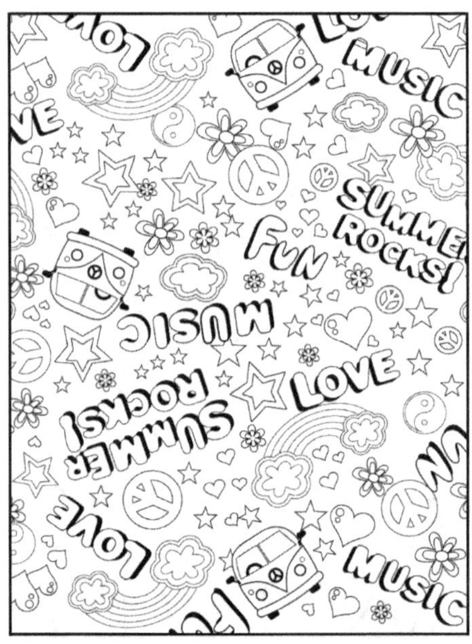

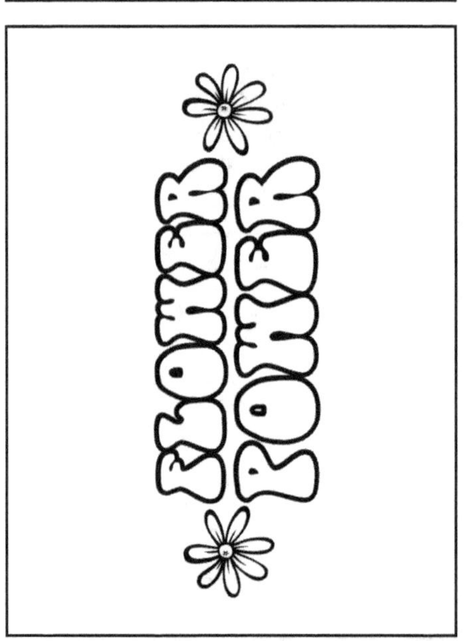

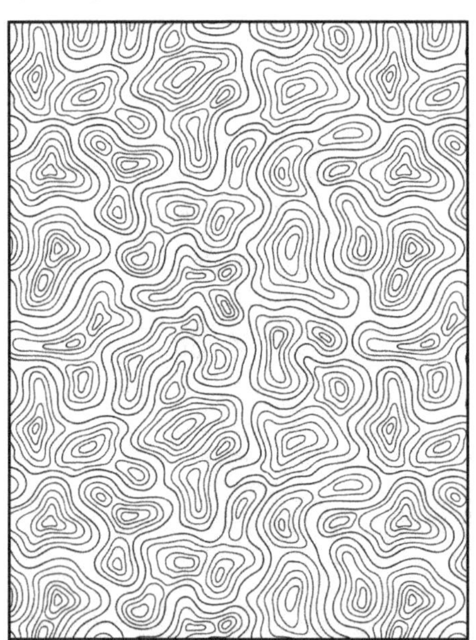

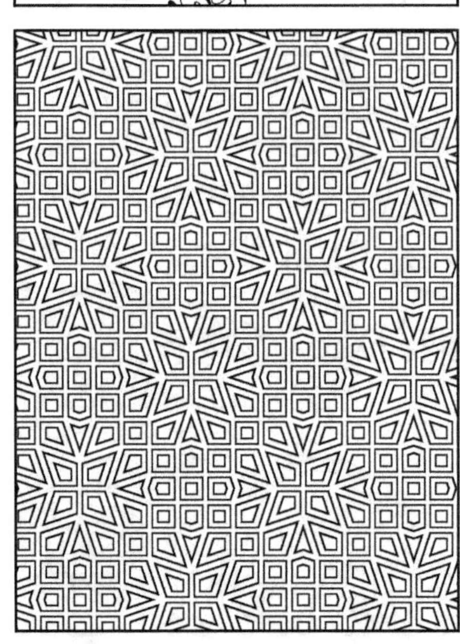

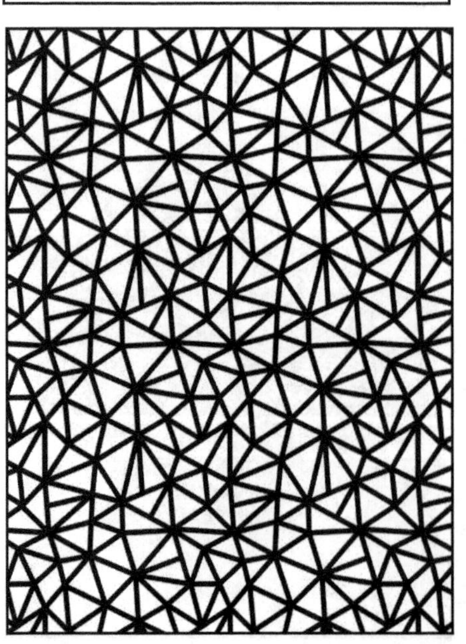

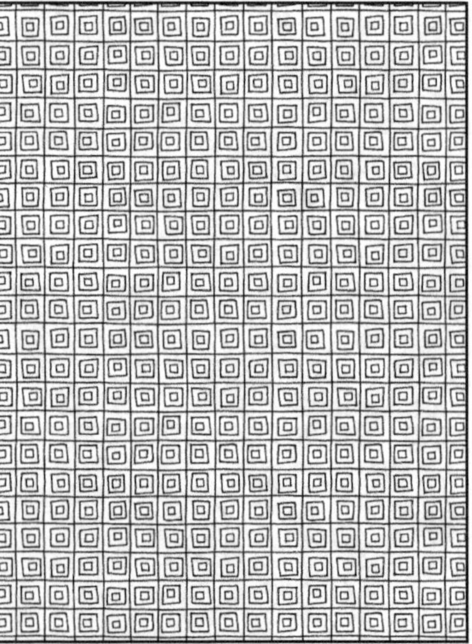

www.arttherapycoloring.com

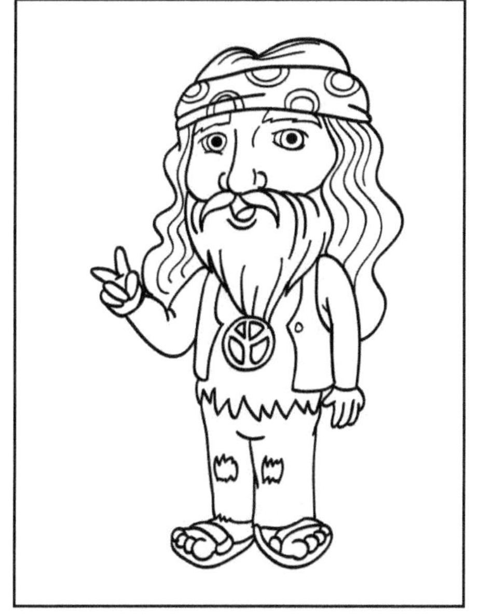

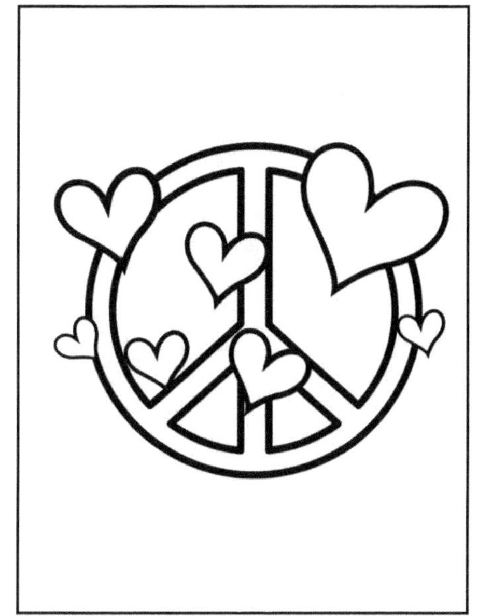

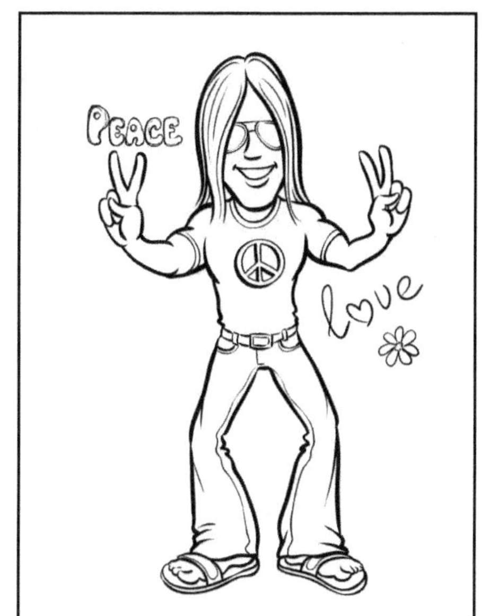

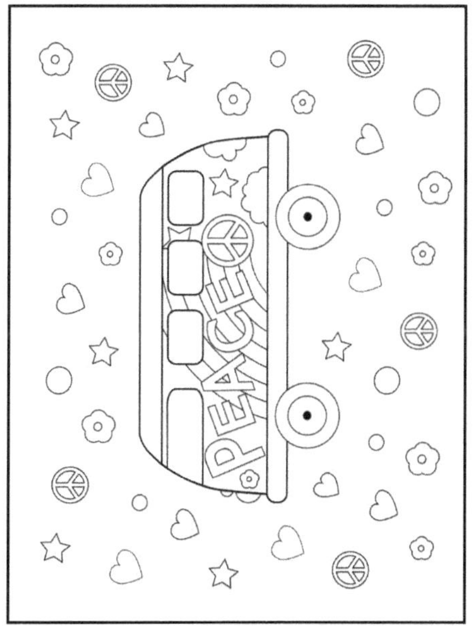

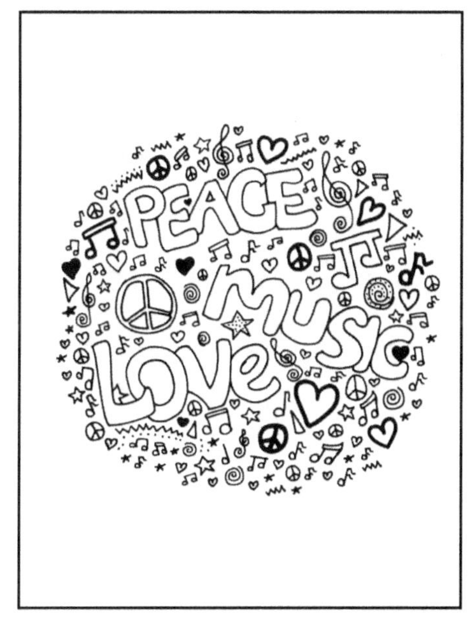

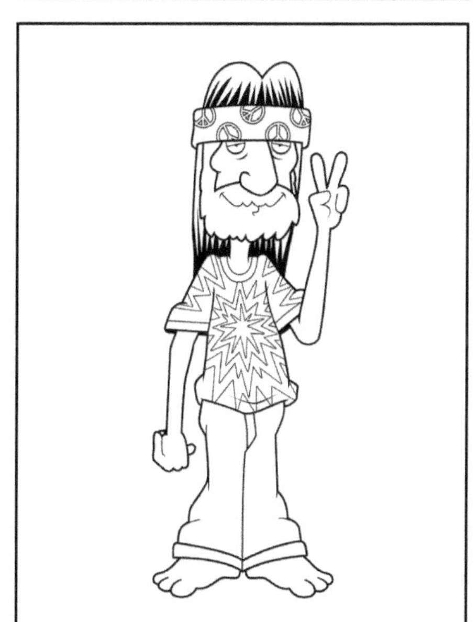

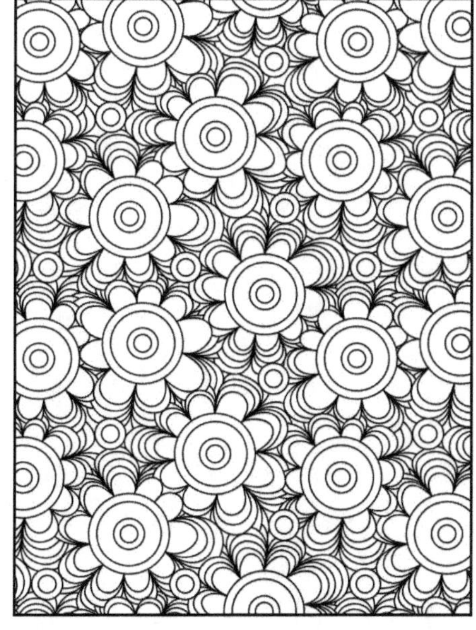

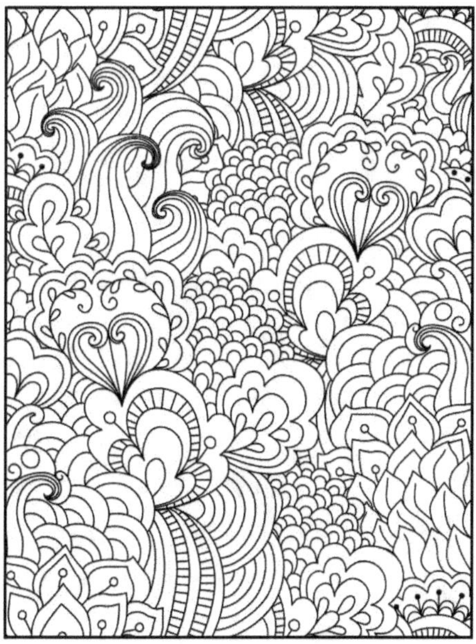

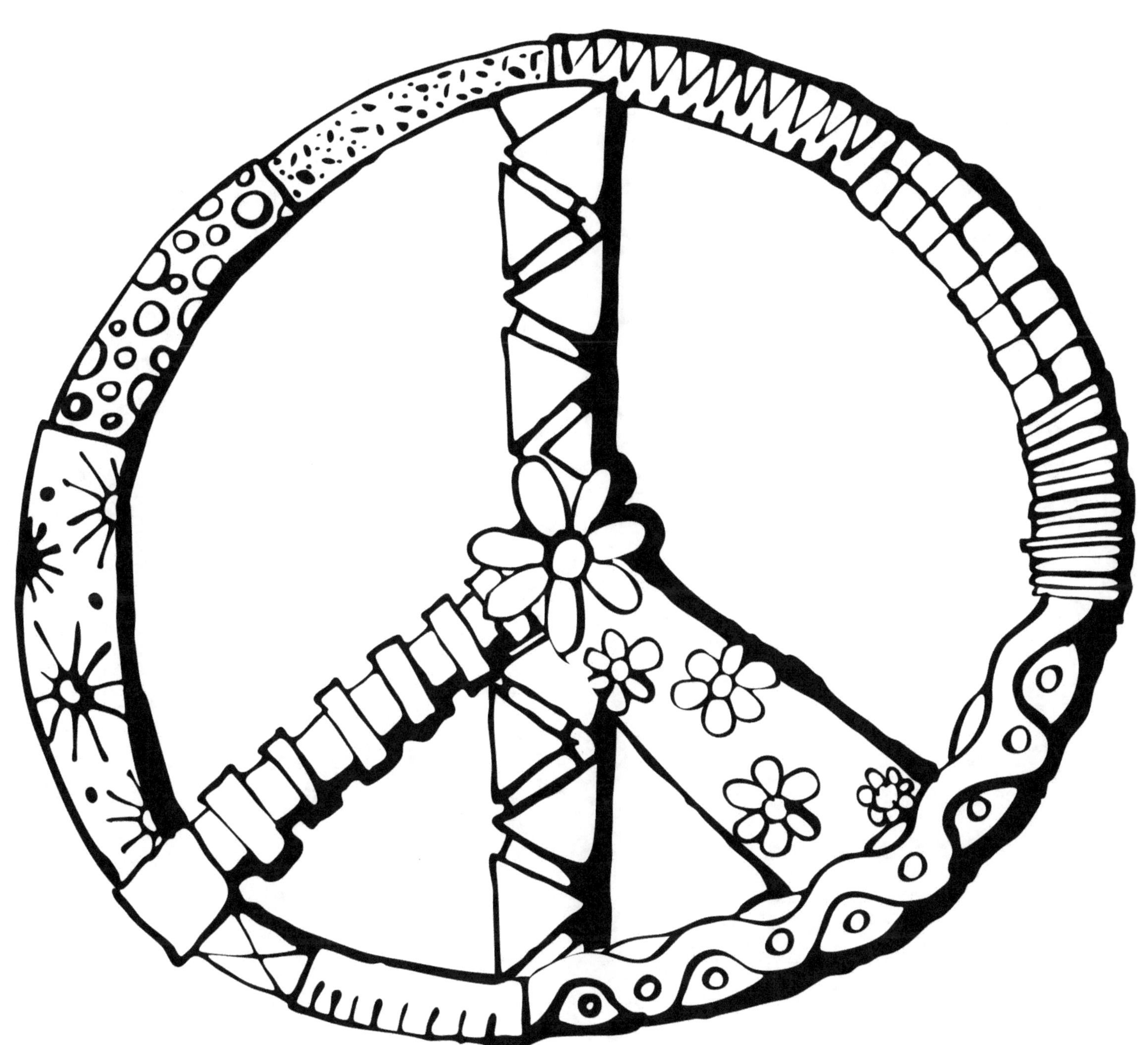

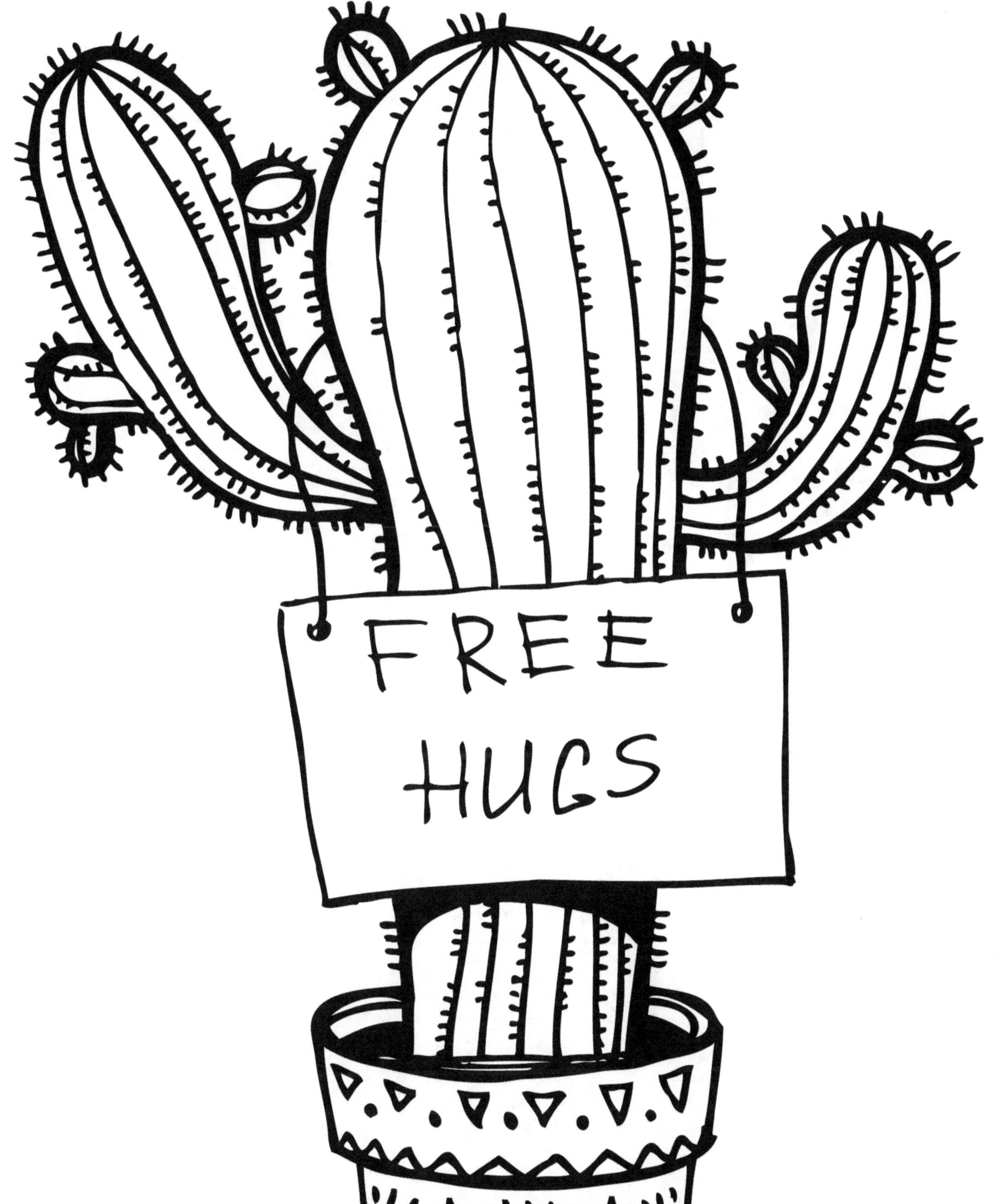
FREE
HUGS

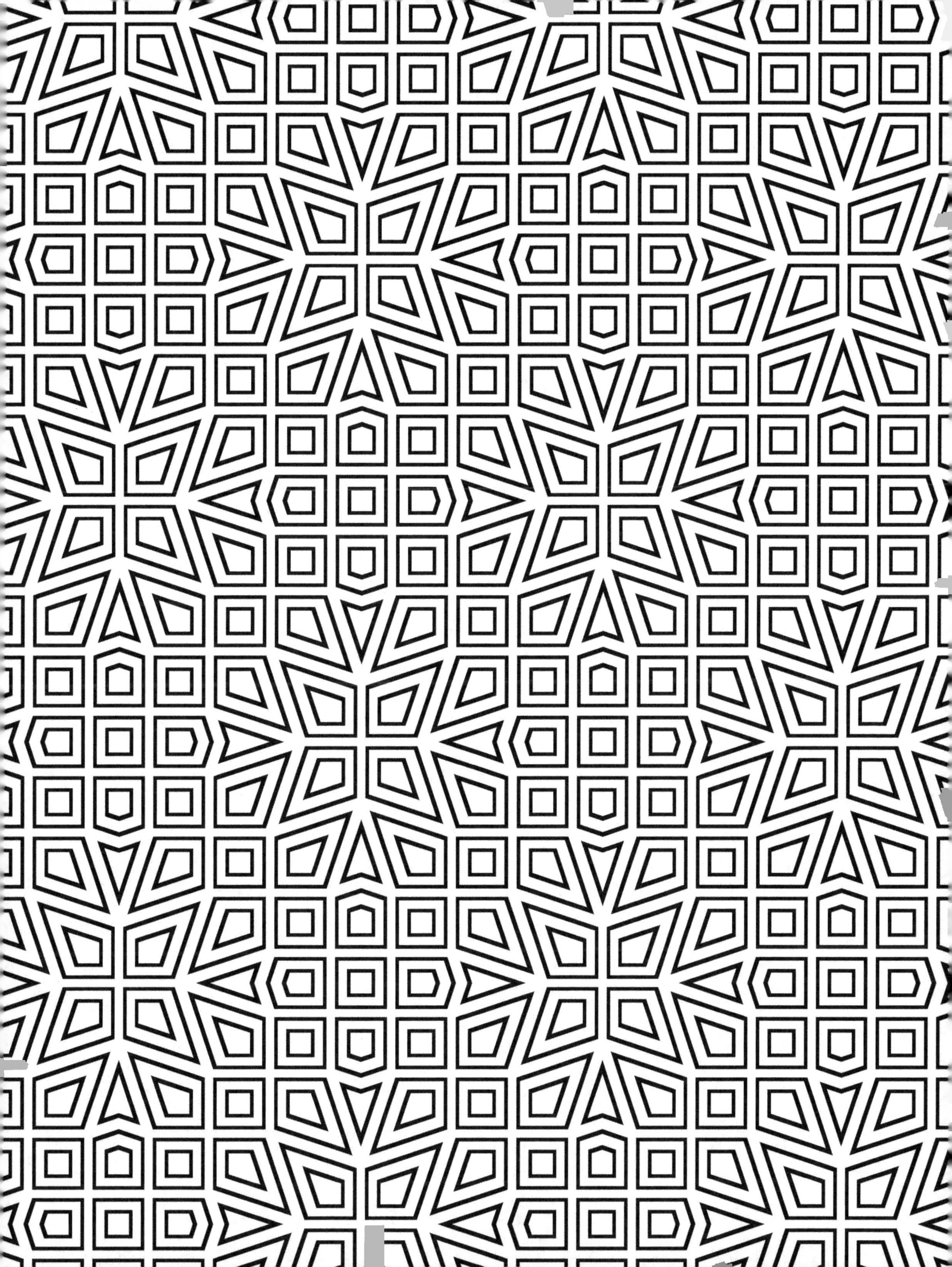

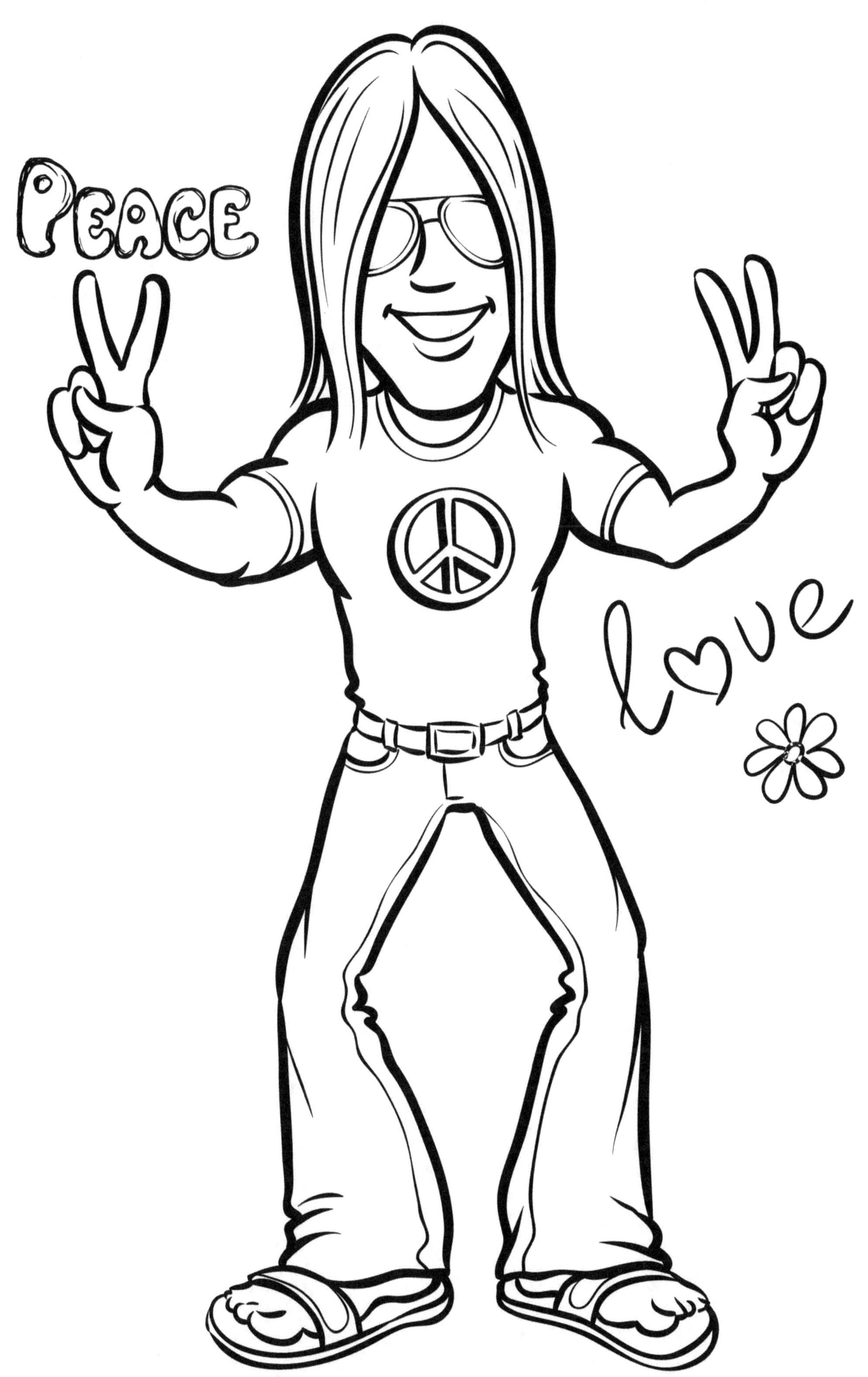
PEACE
Love

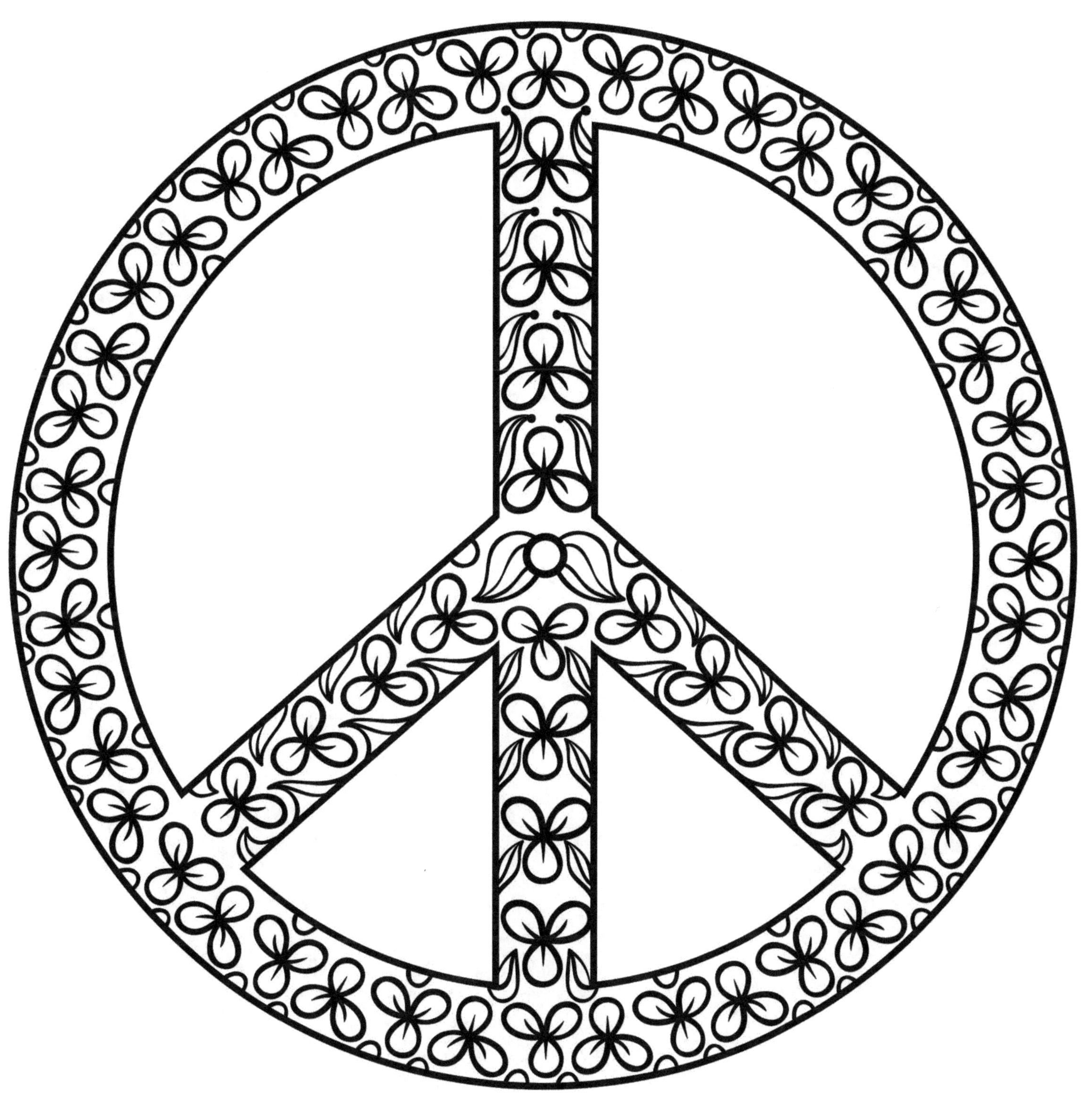

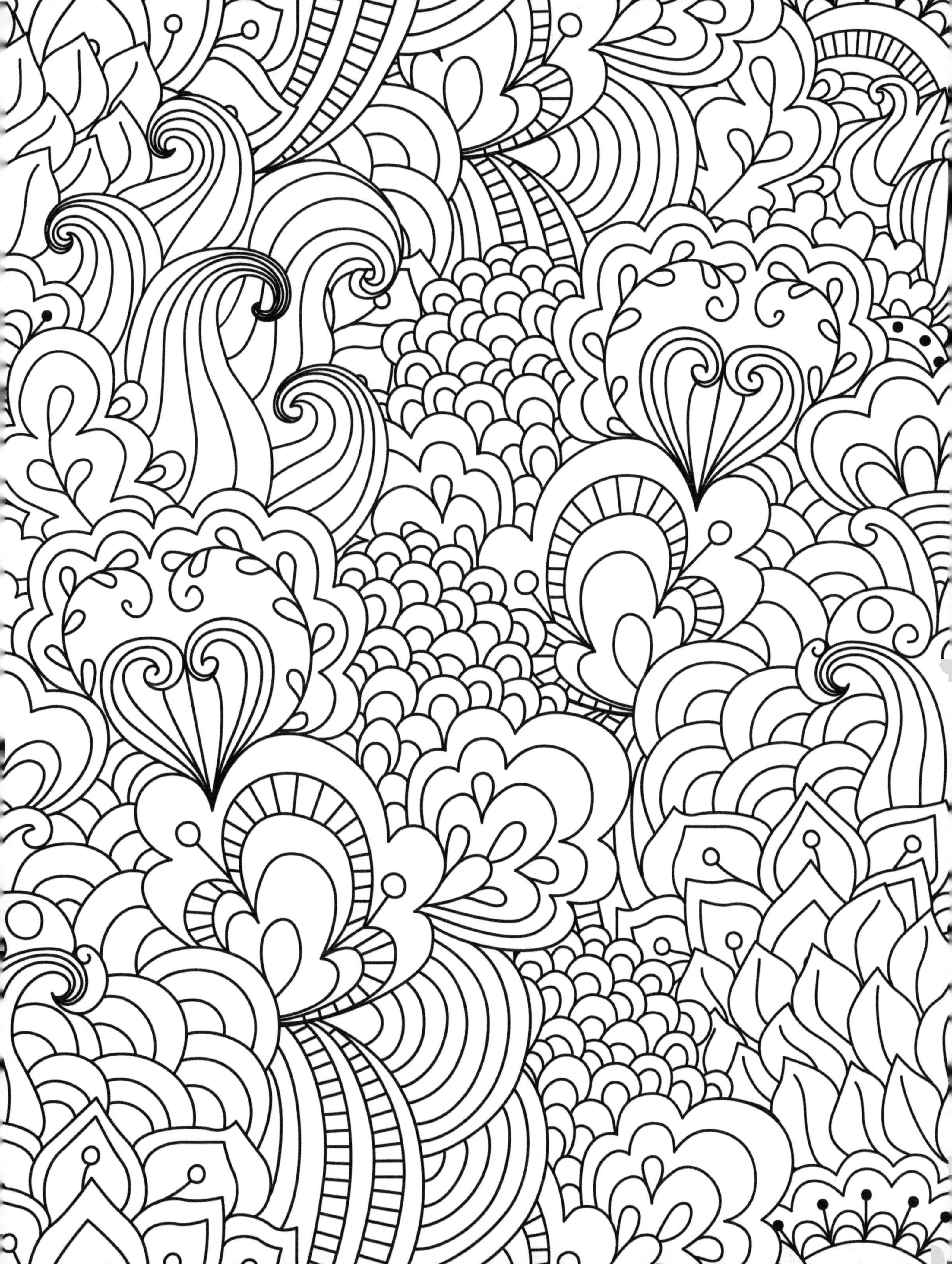

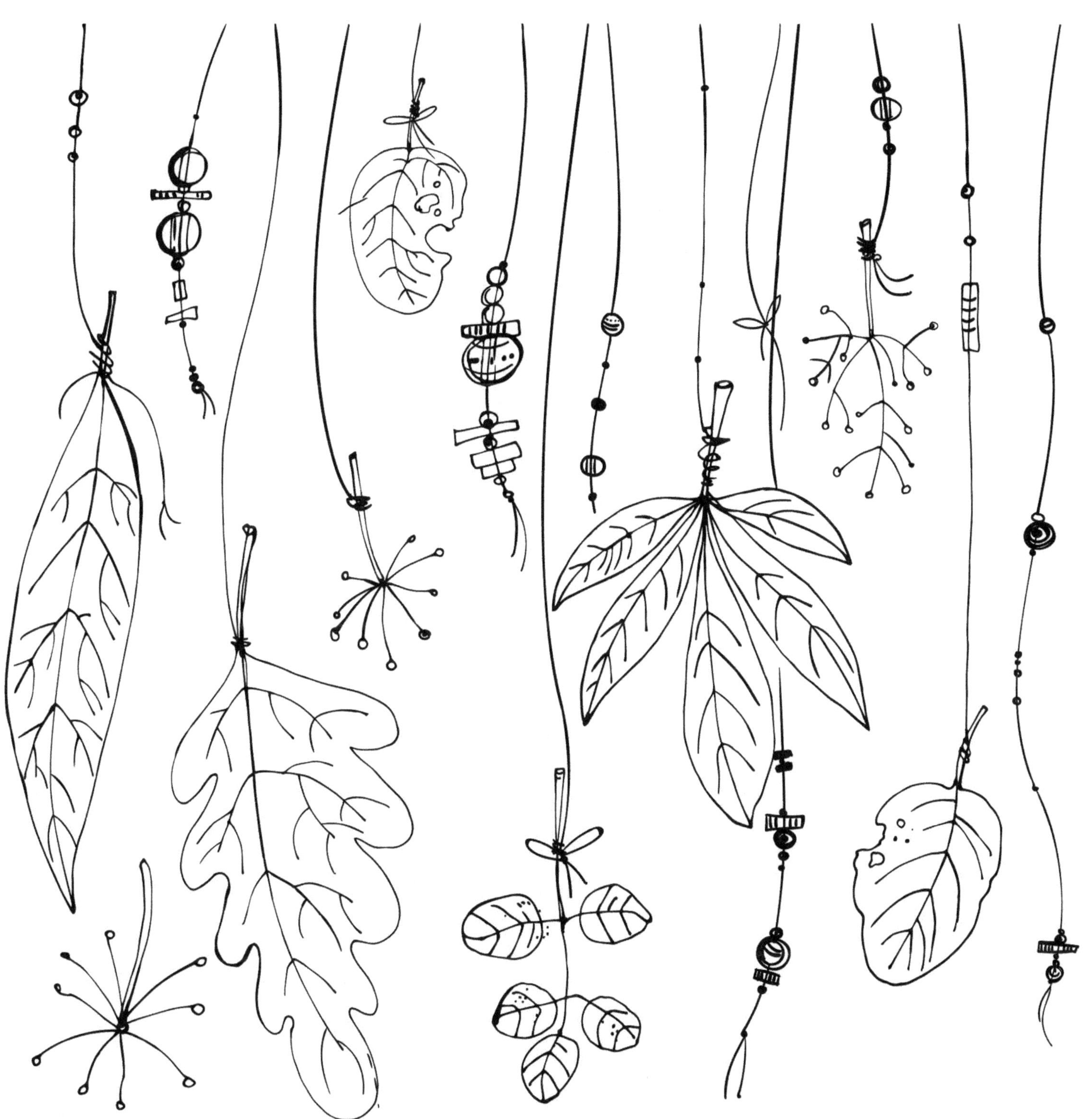

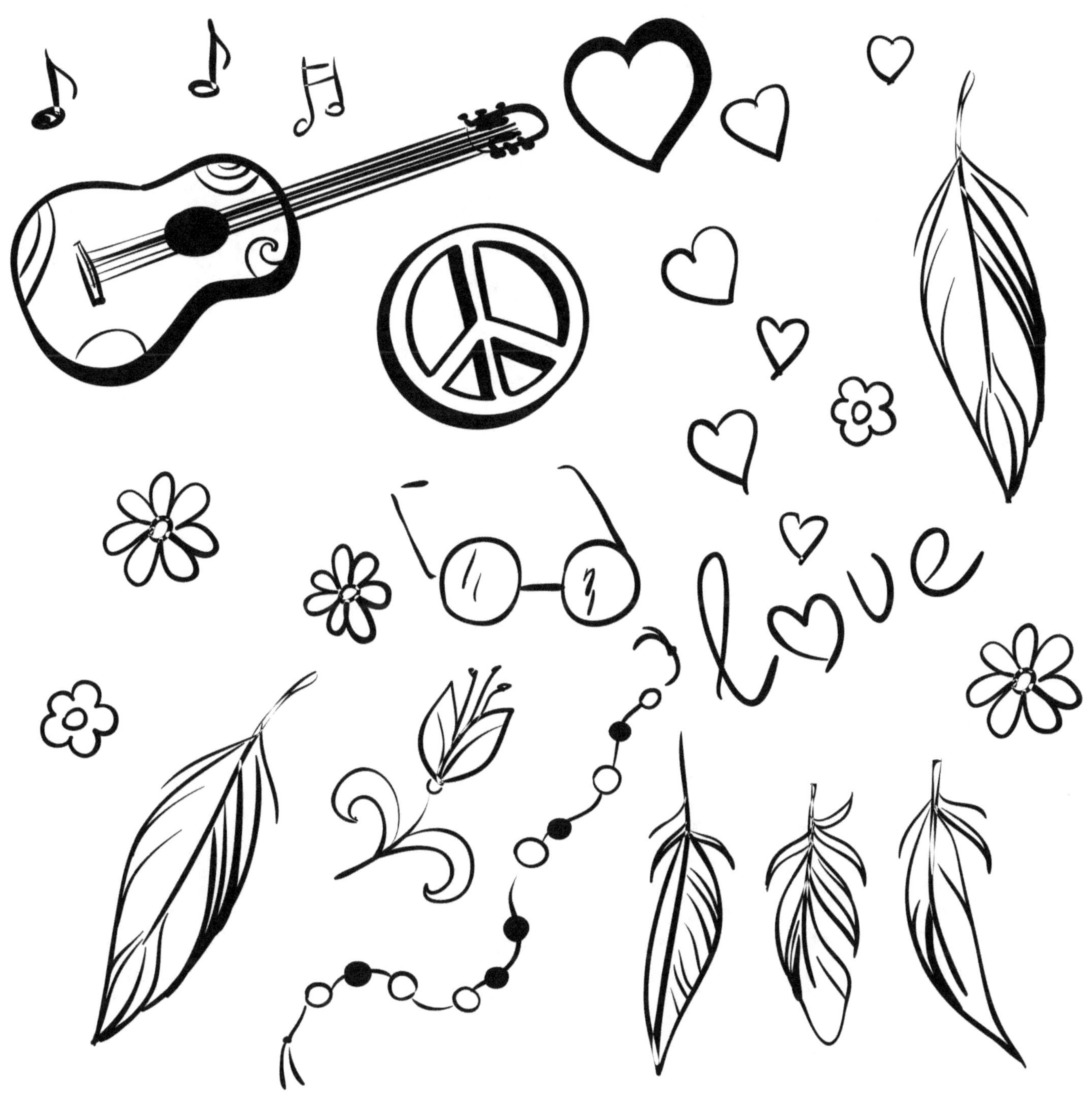
love

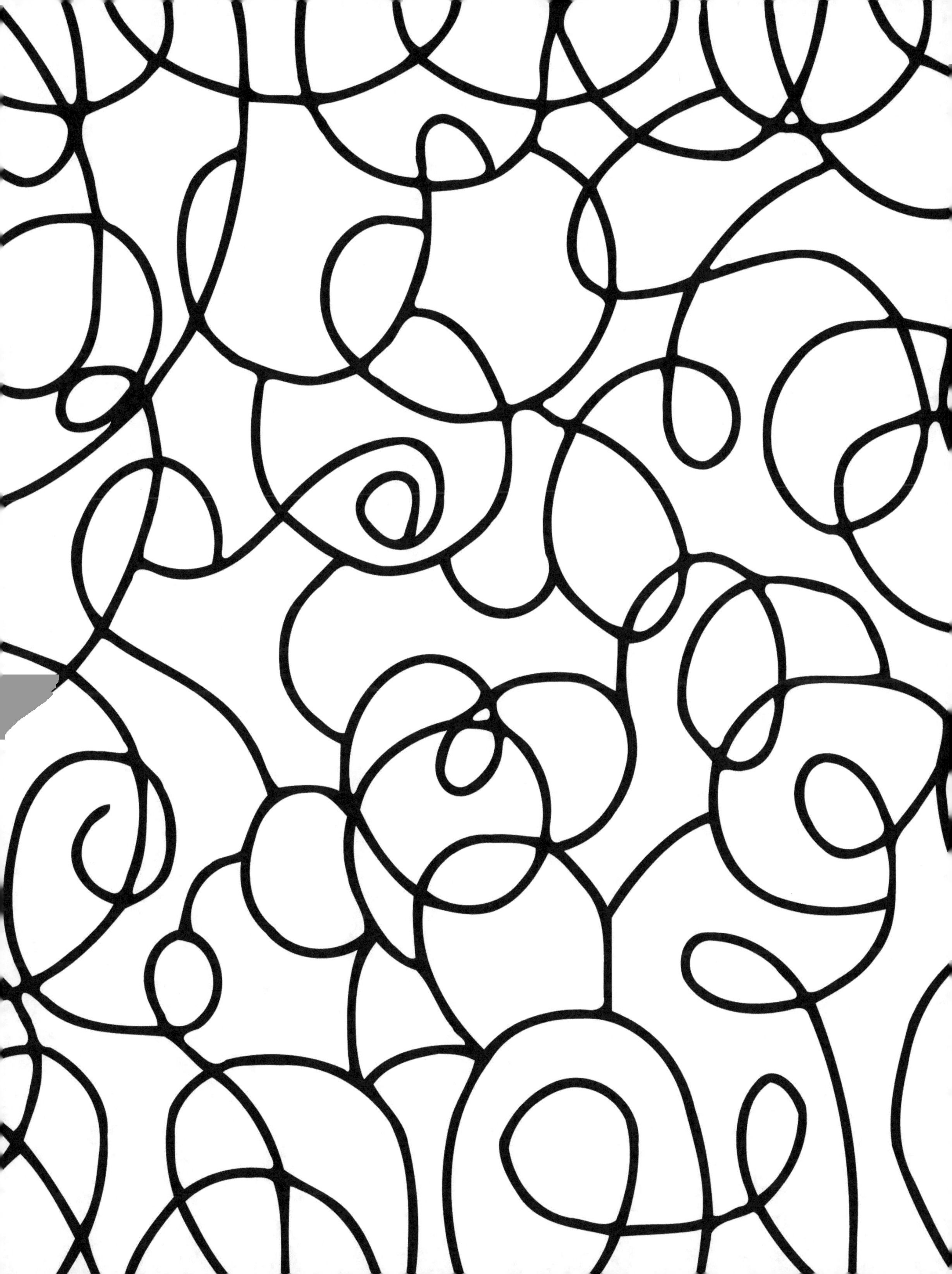

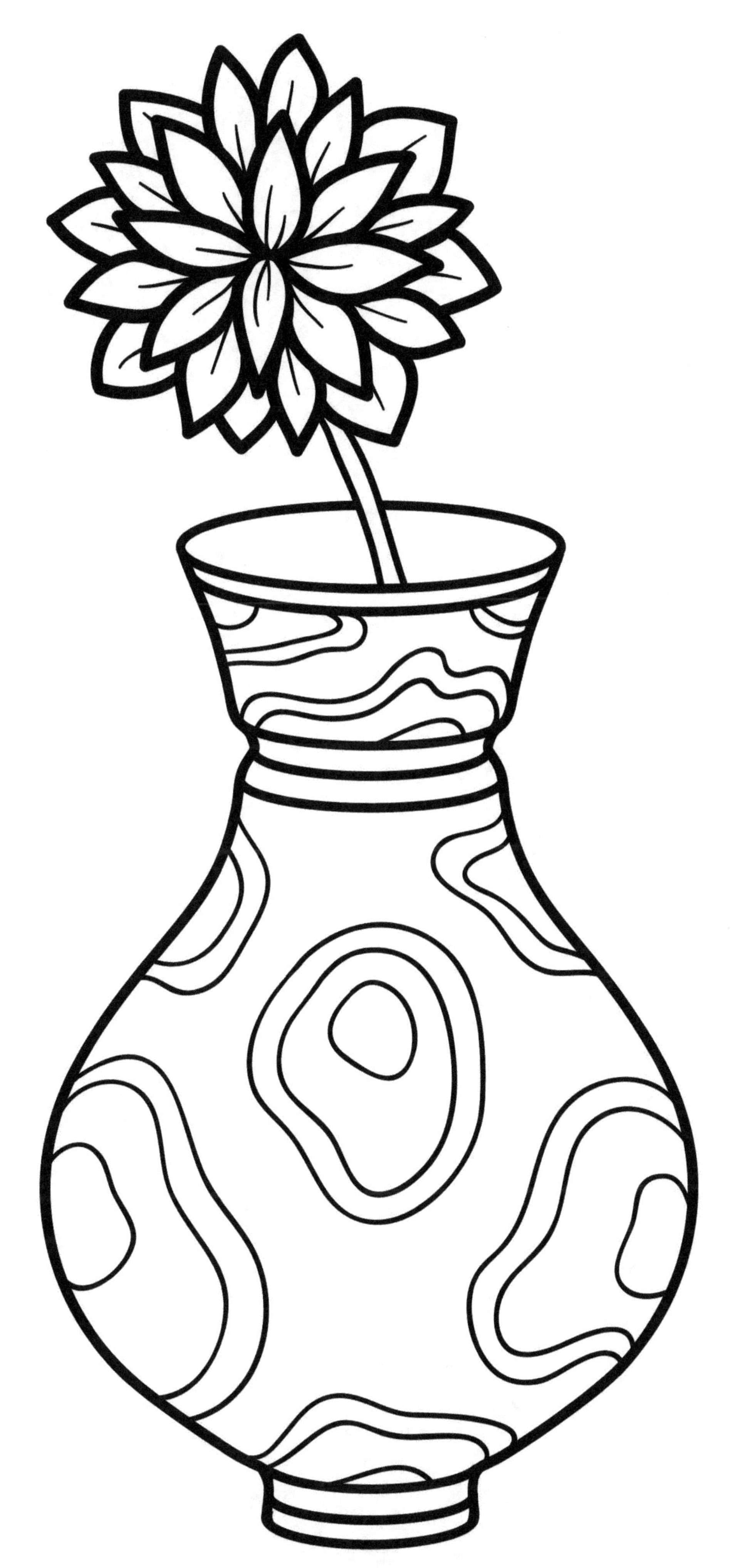

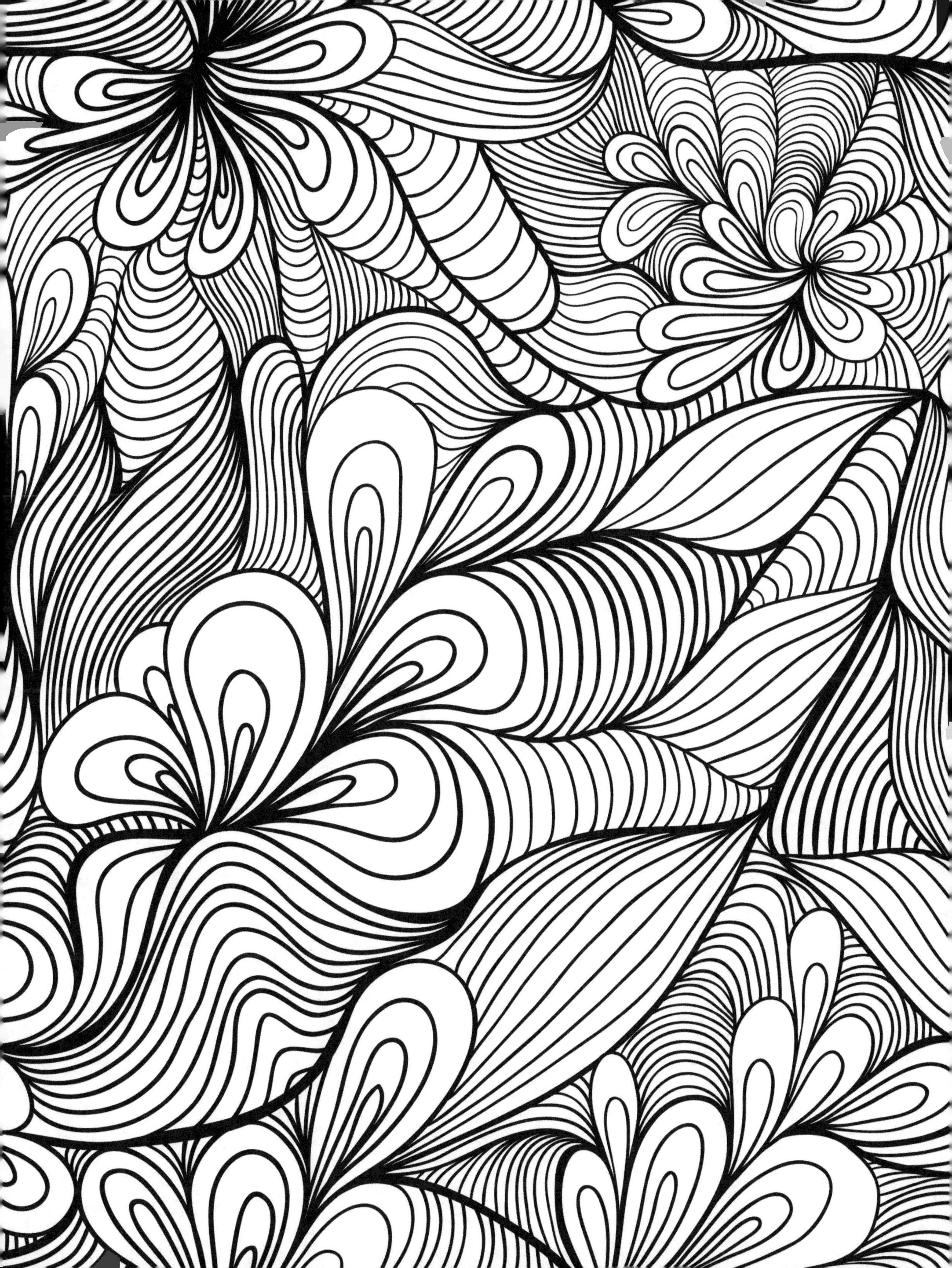

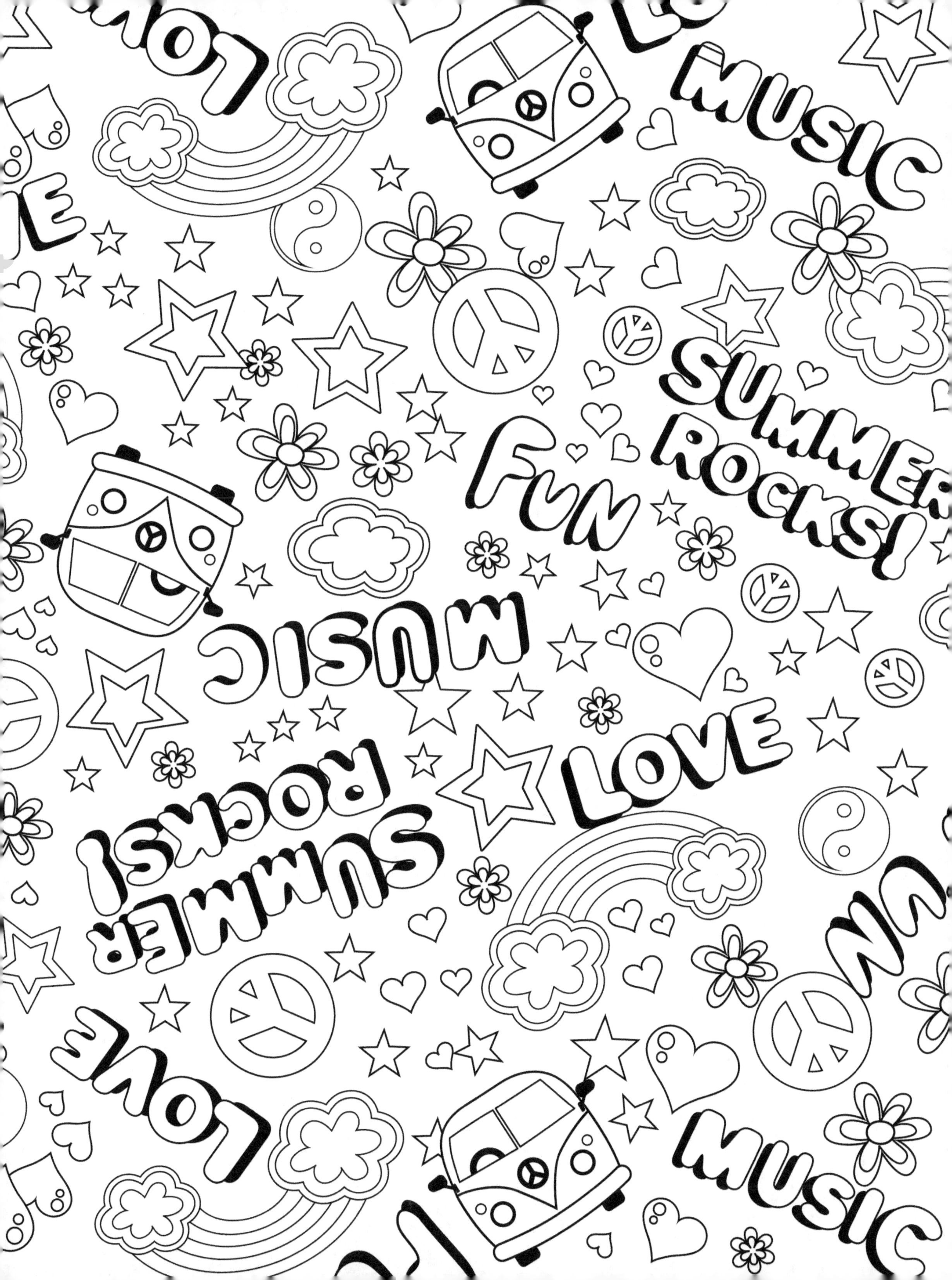
LOVE
MUSIC
SUMMER ROCKS!
FUN

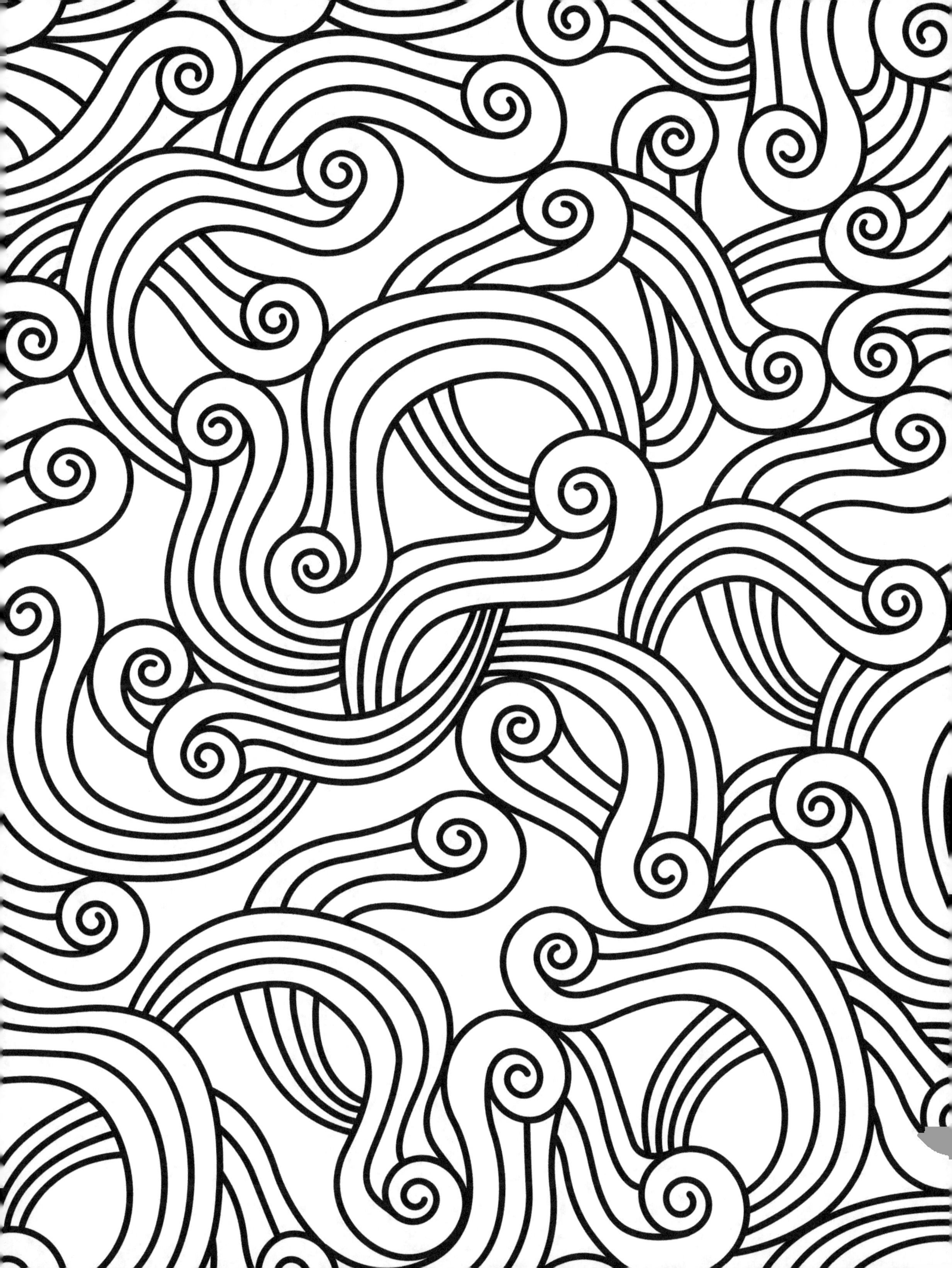

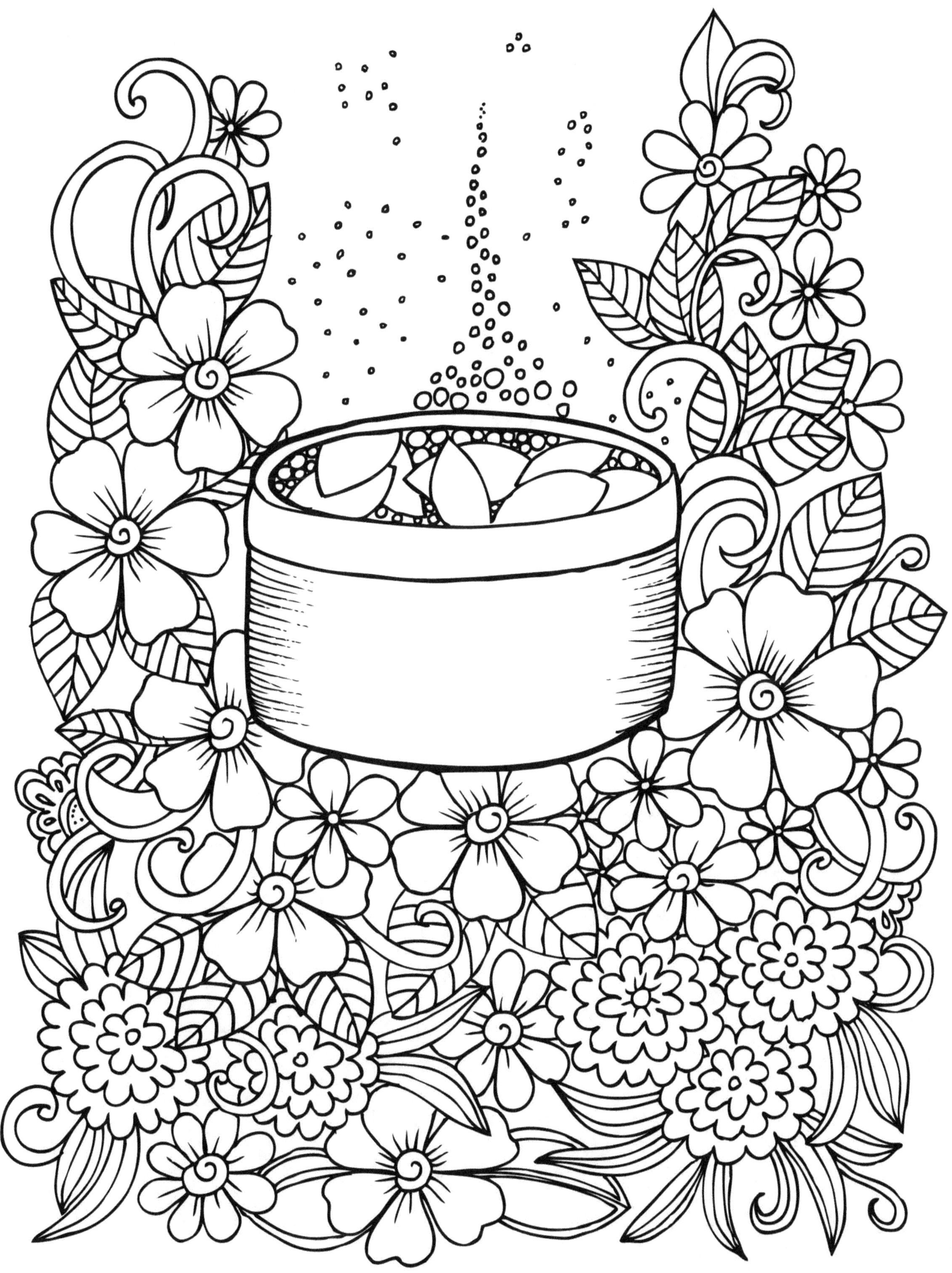

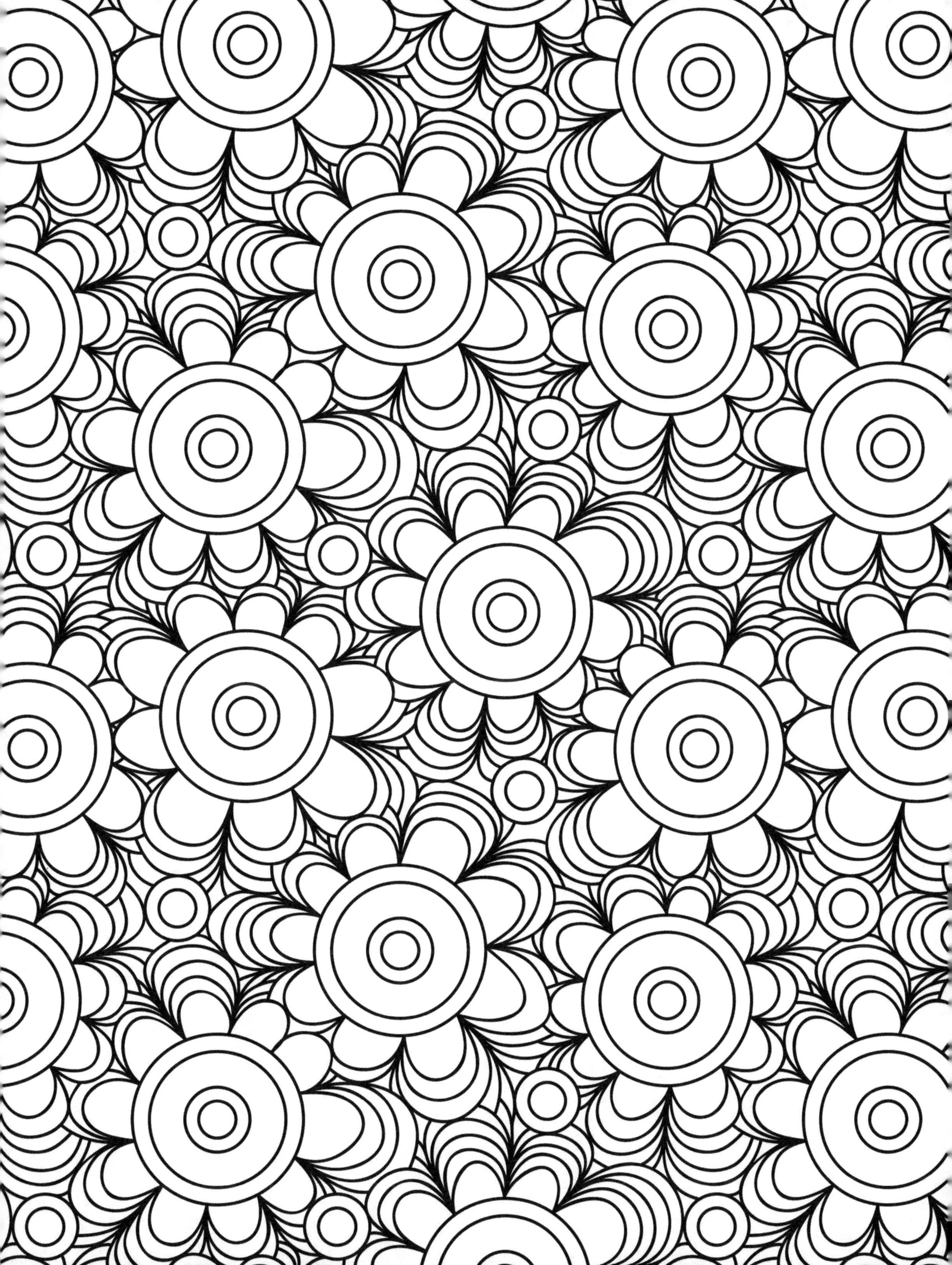

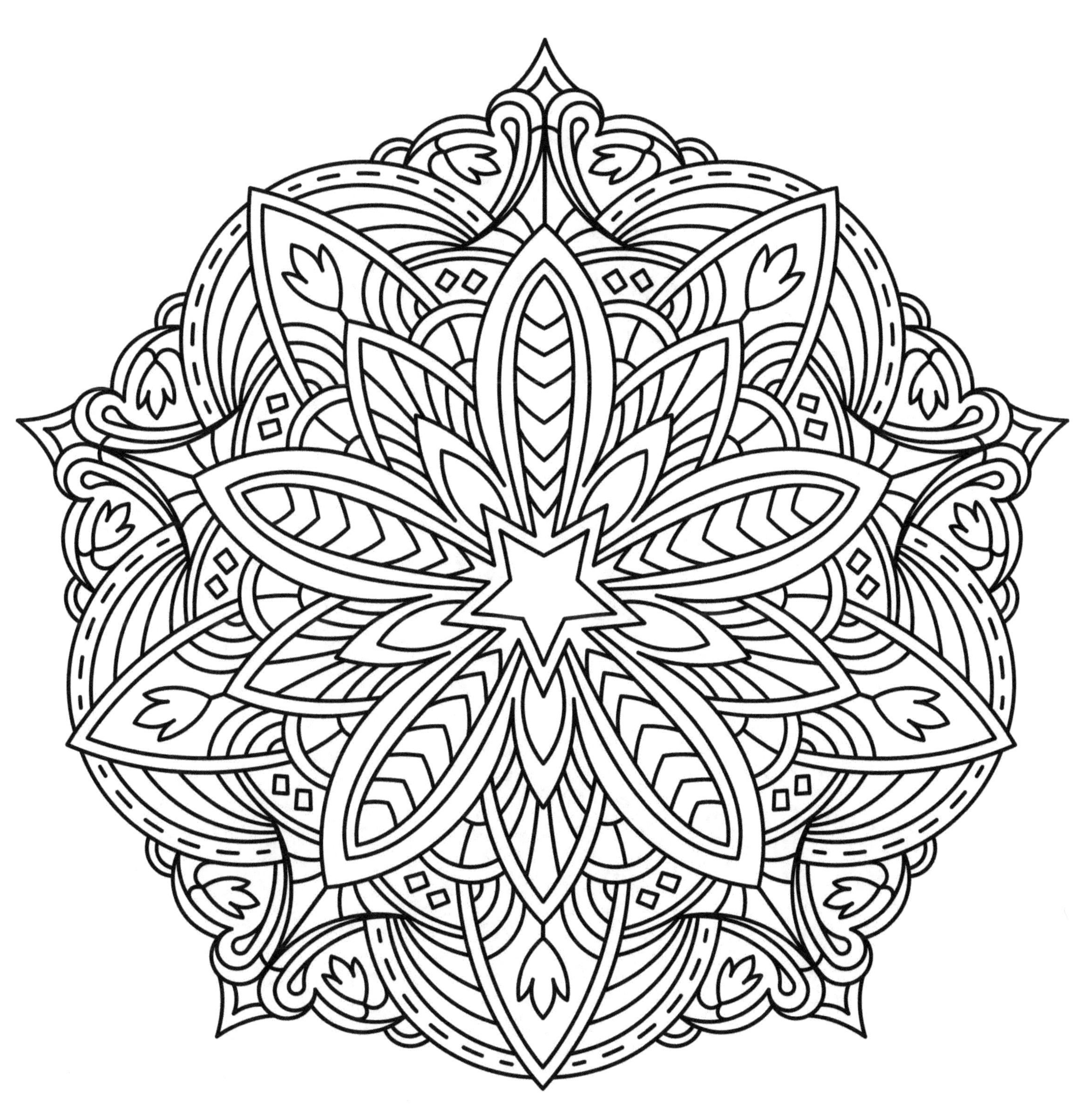

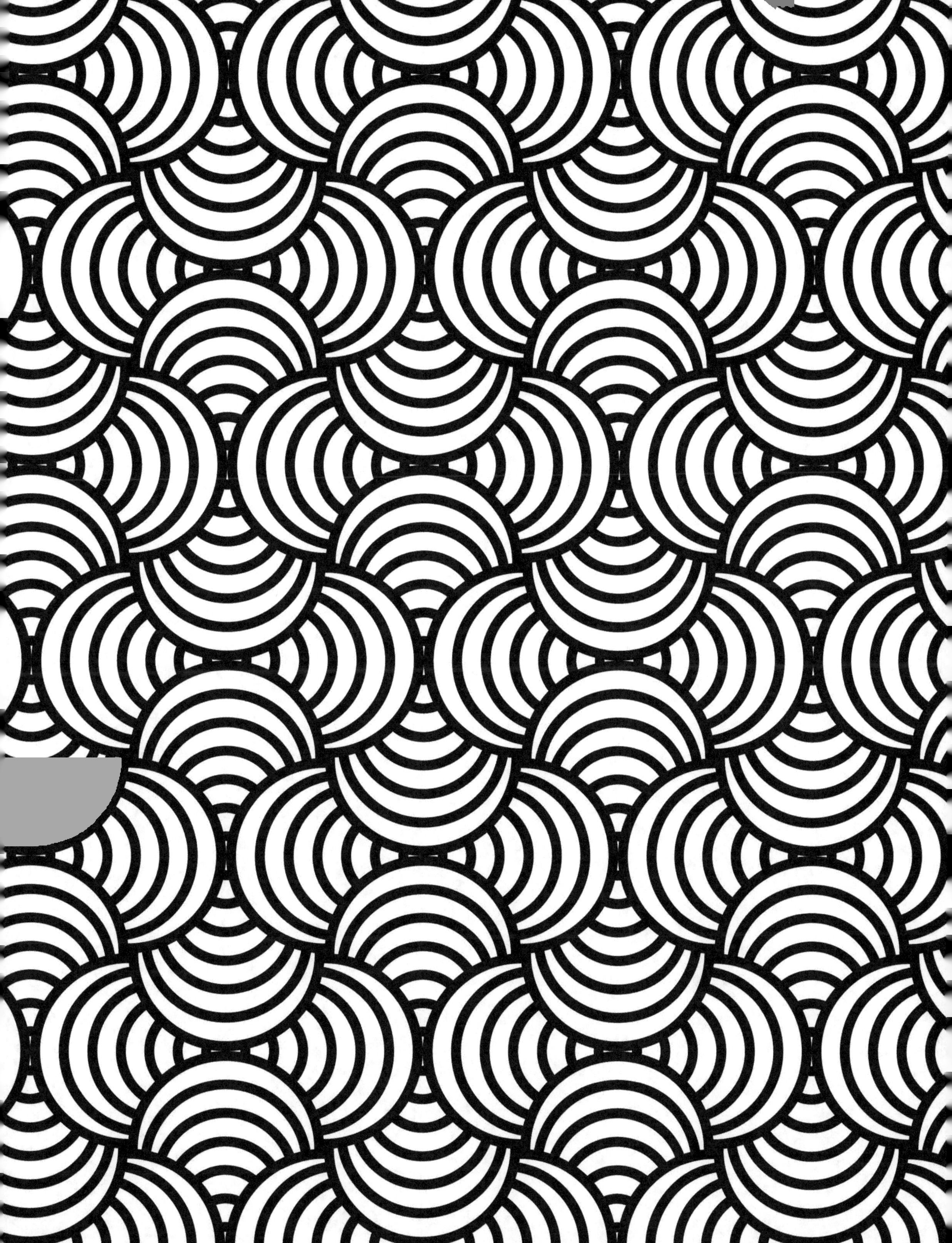

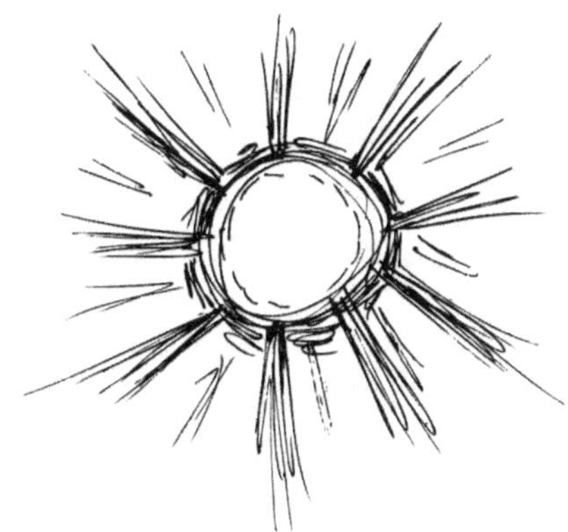

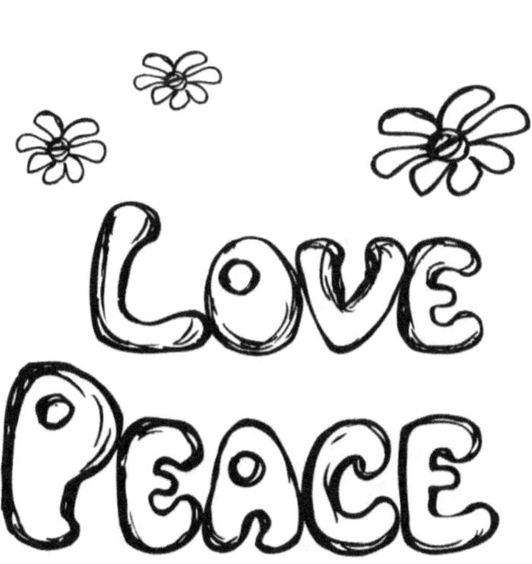
LOVE
PEACE

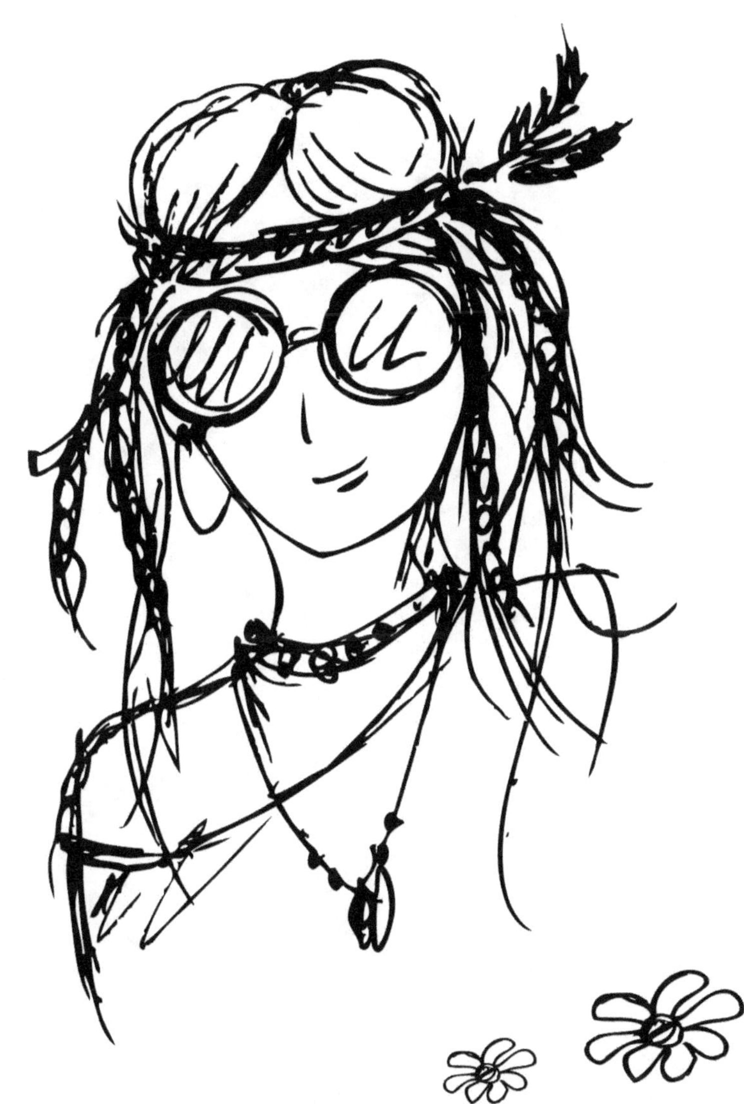

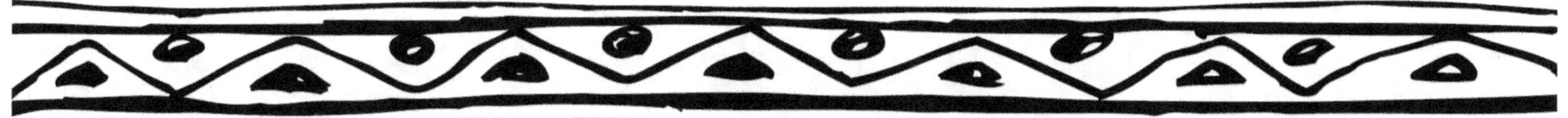

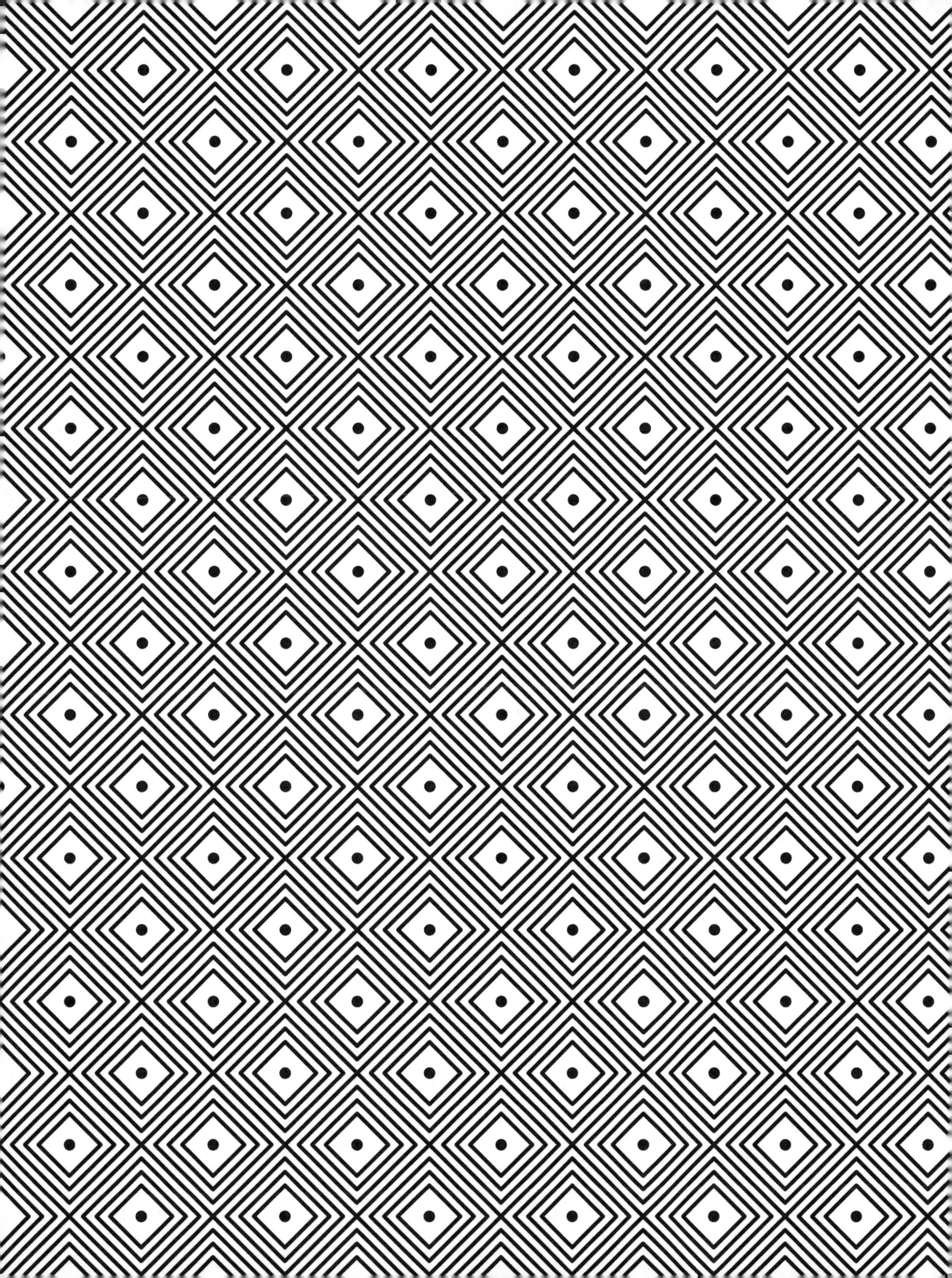

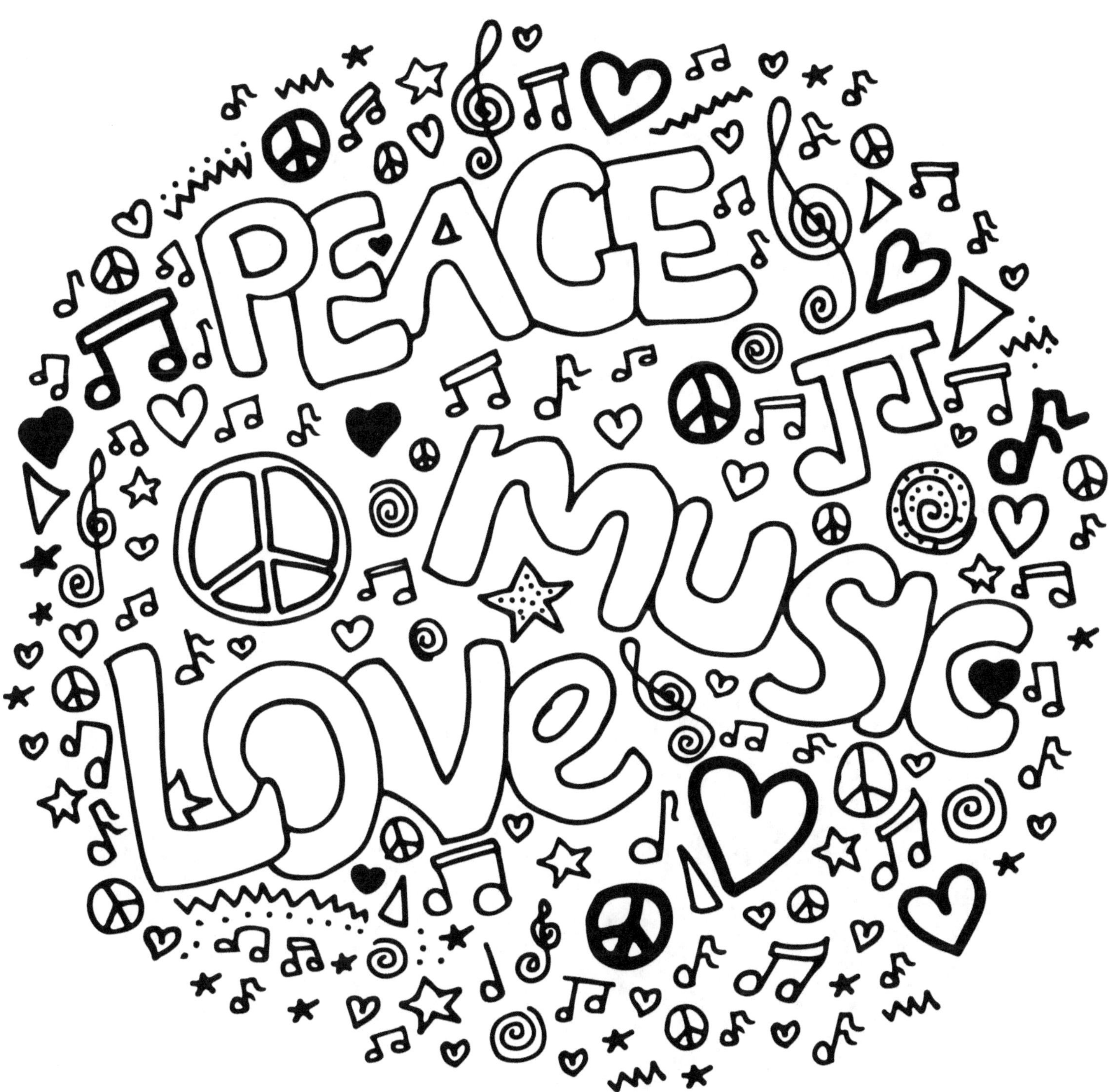
PEACE
MUSIC
LOVE

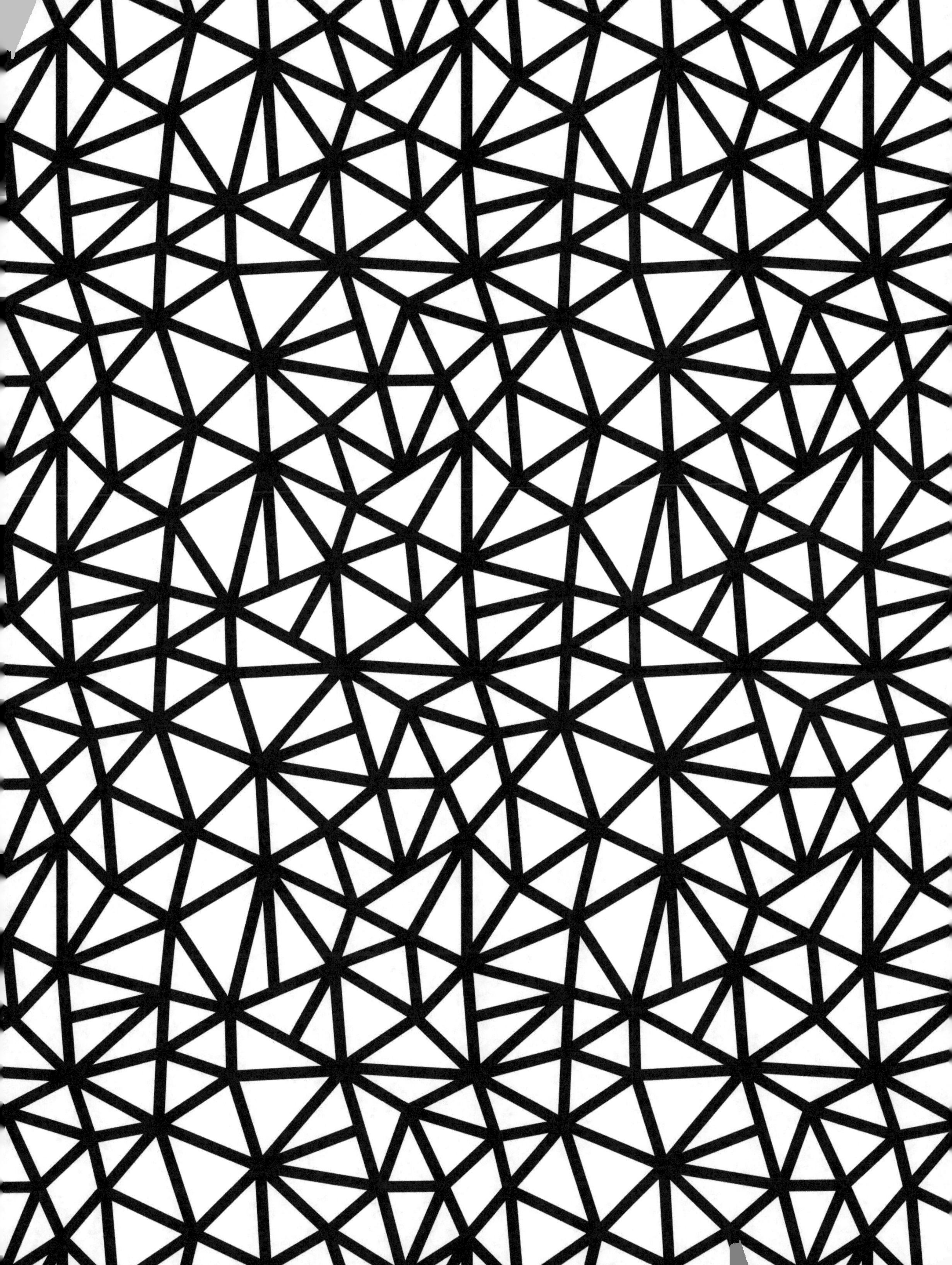

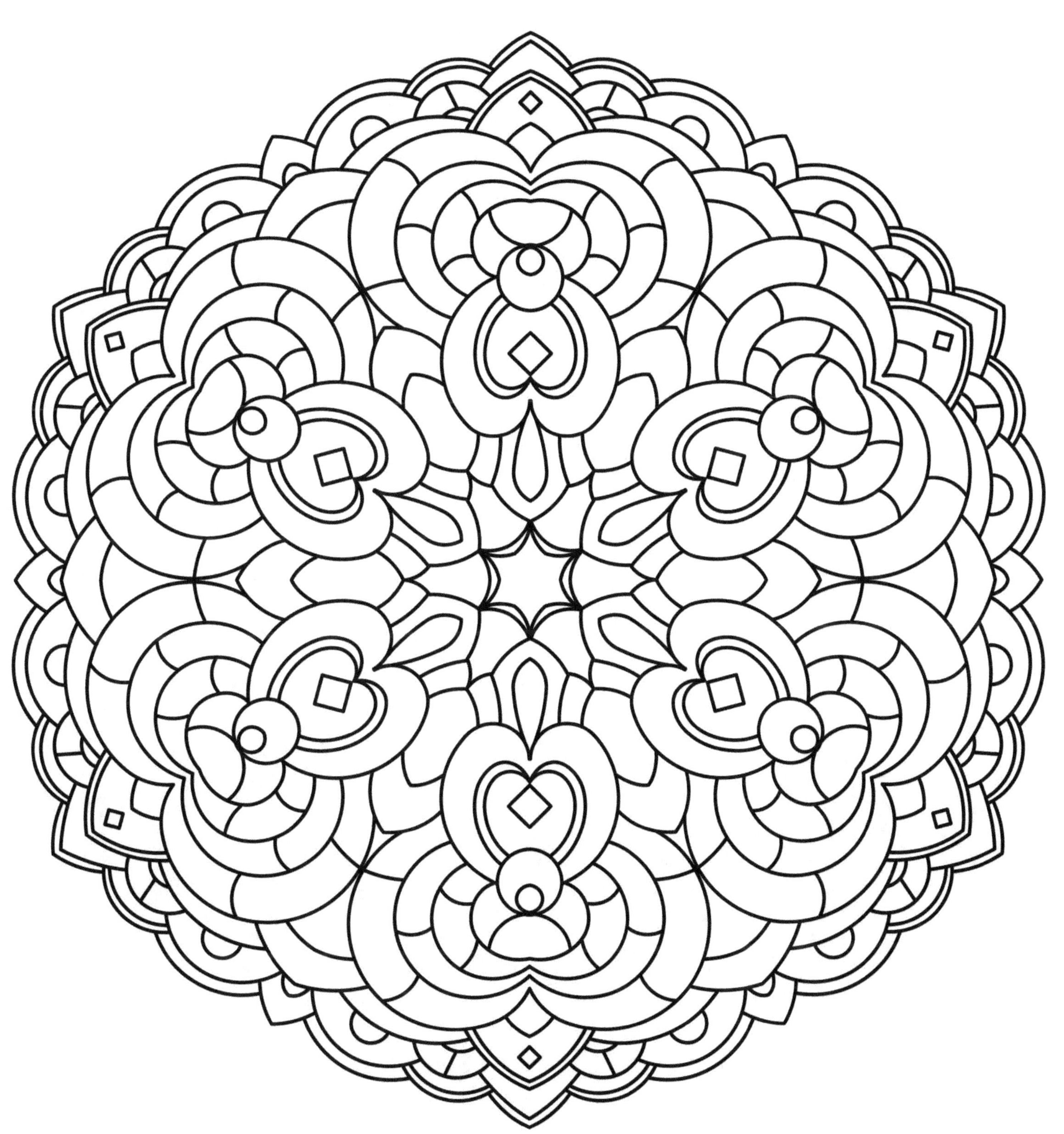

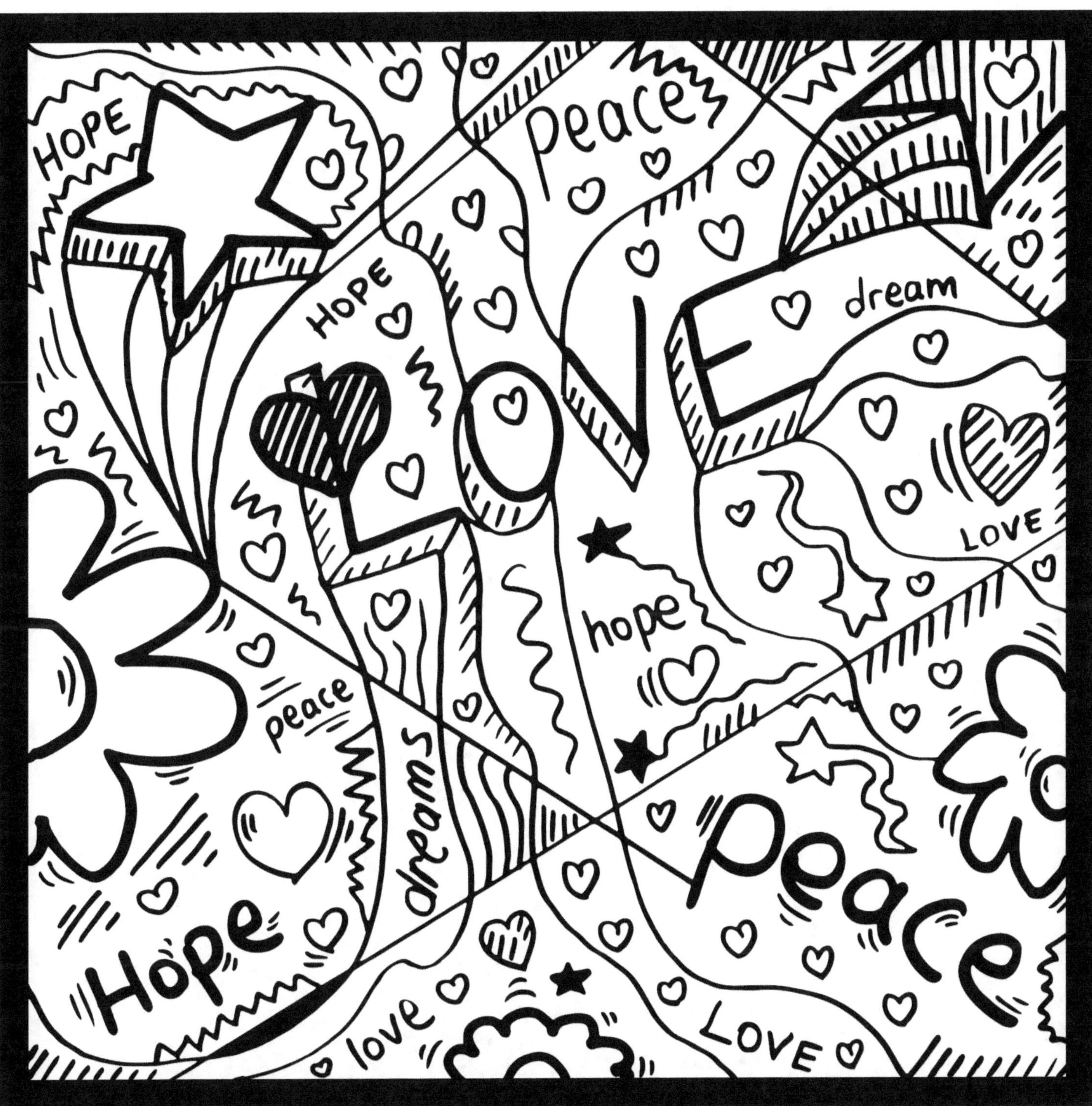
HOPE
peace
HOPE
LOVE
dream
LOVE
hope
peace
dreams
Hope
Peace
love
LOVE

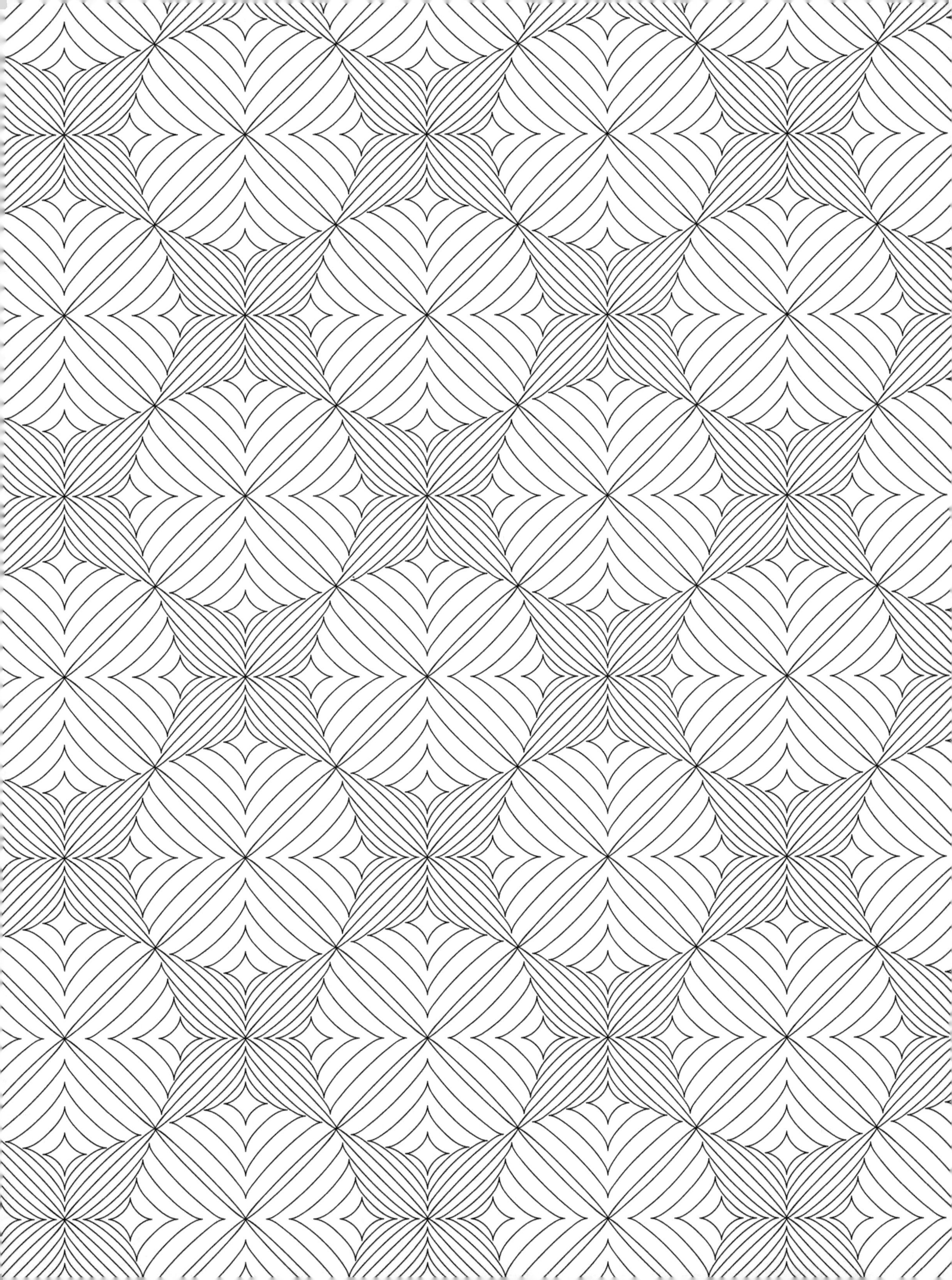

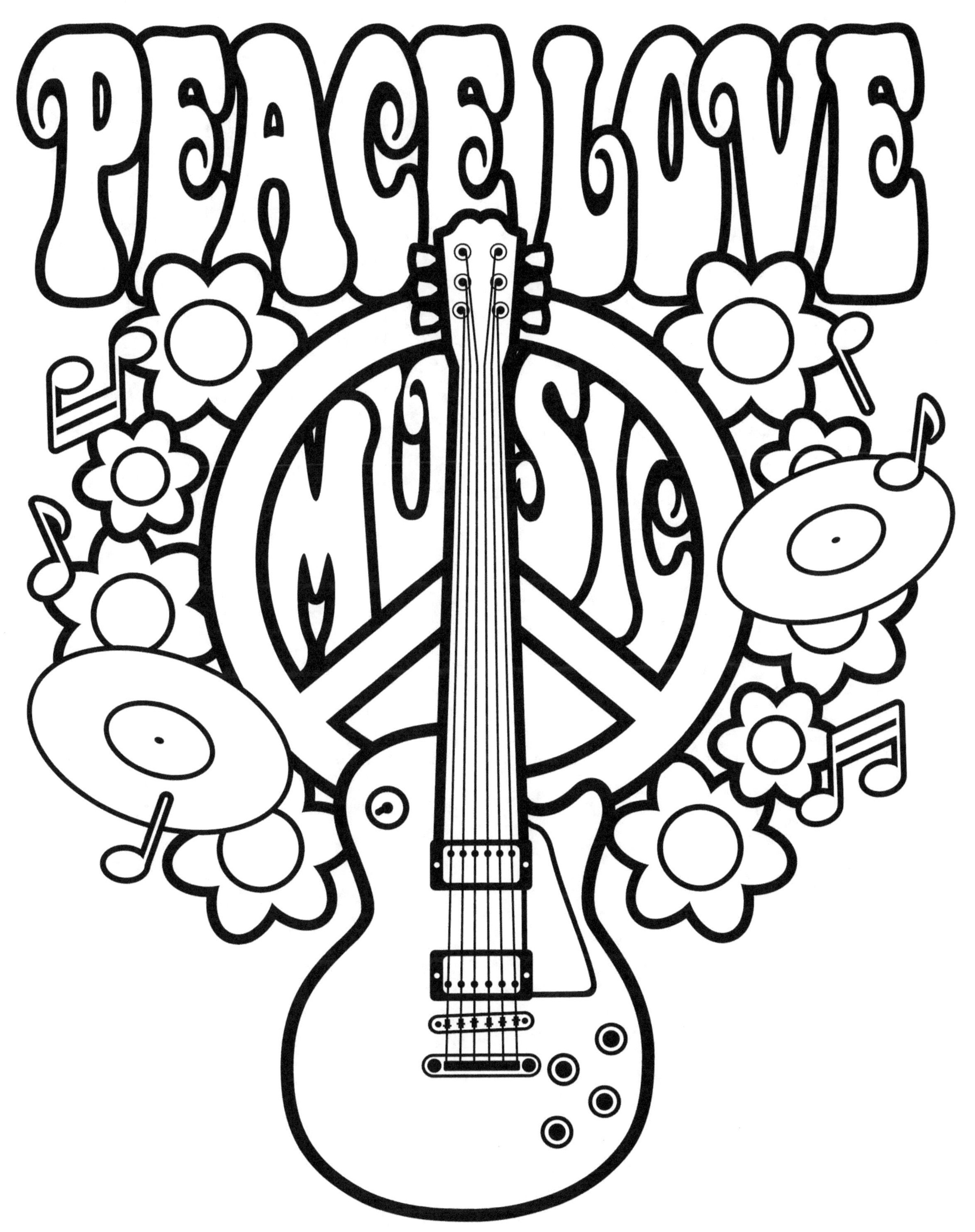
PEACE LOVE
MUSIC

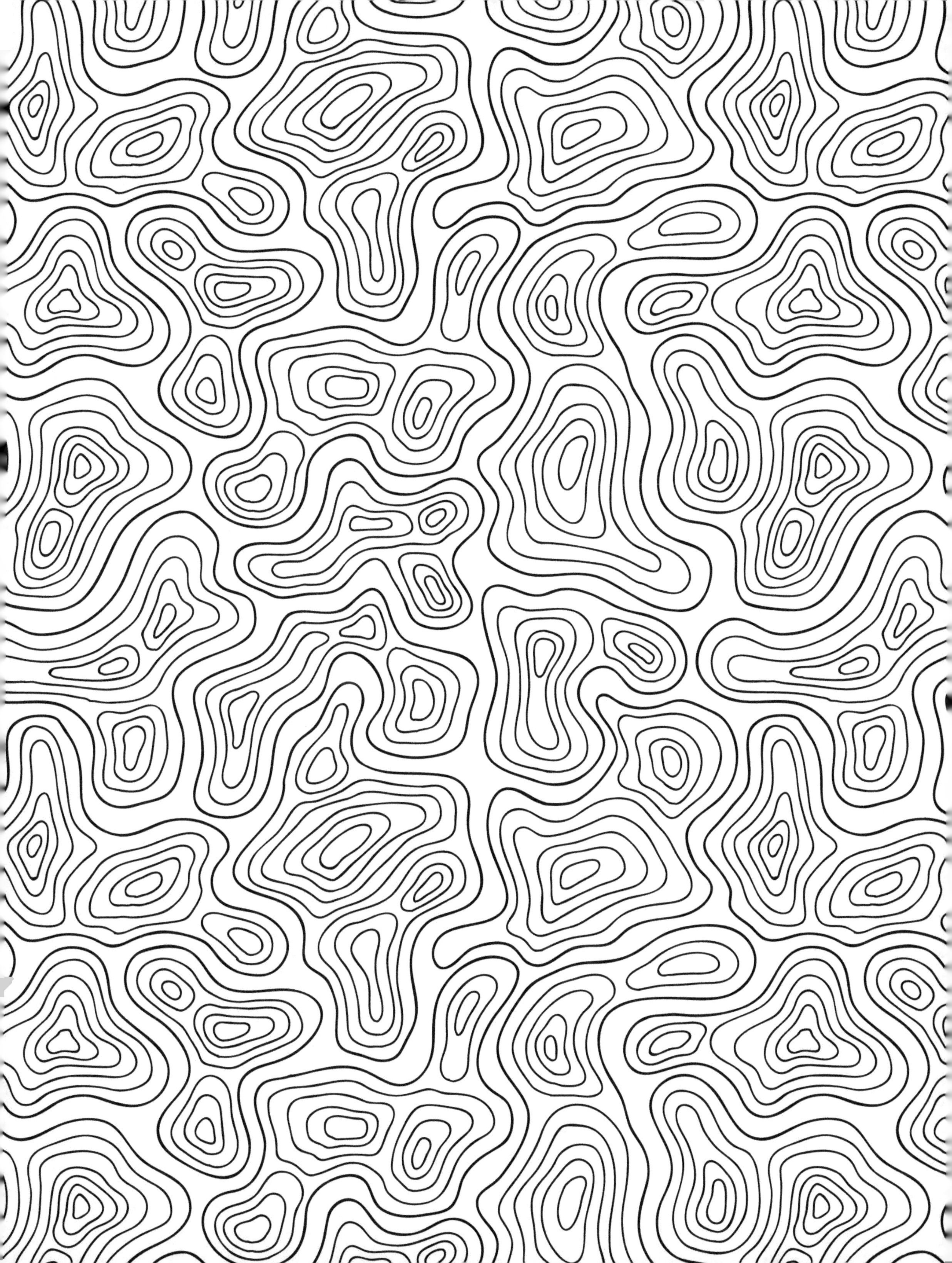

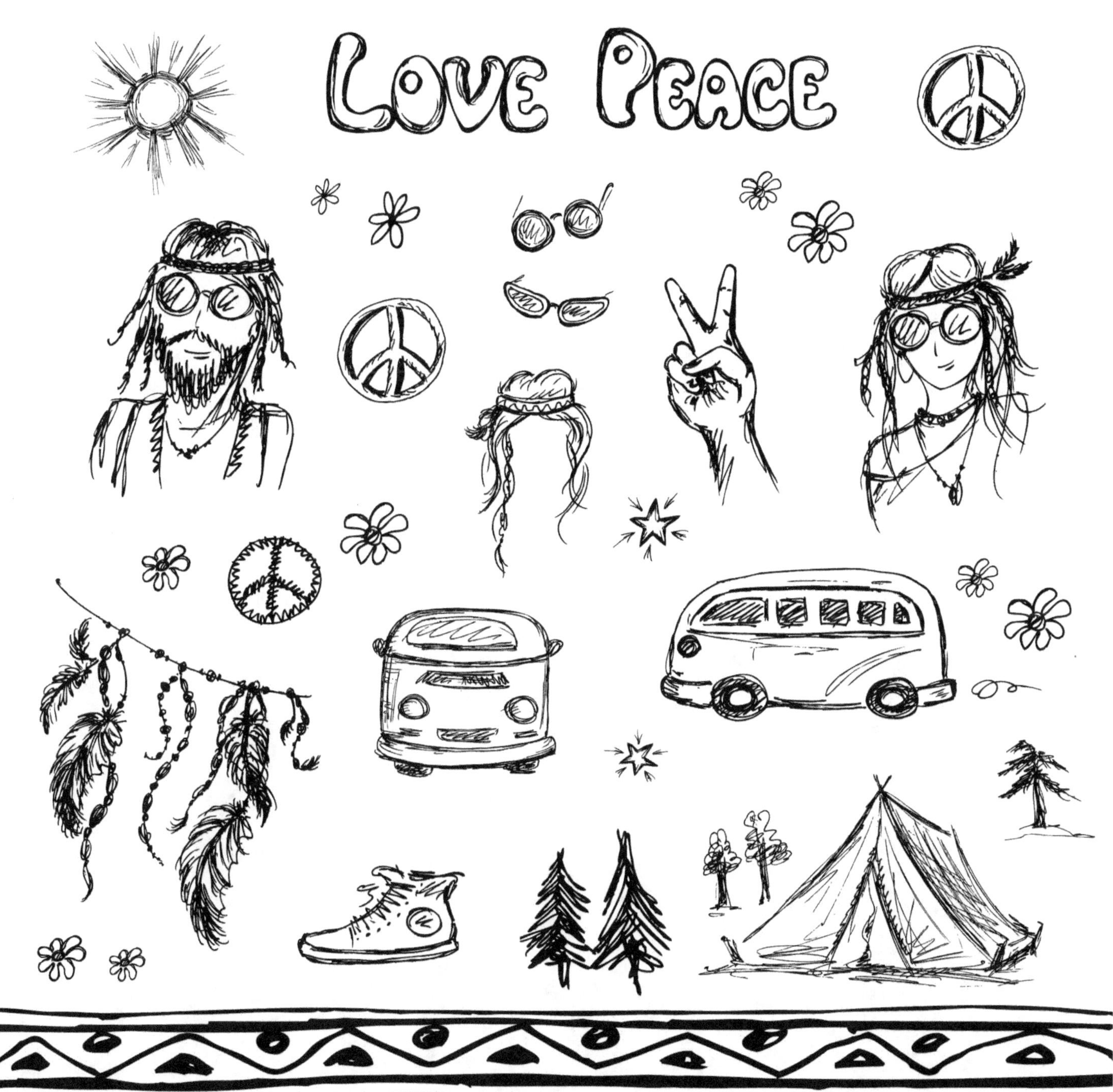
LOVE PEACE

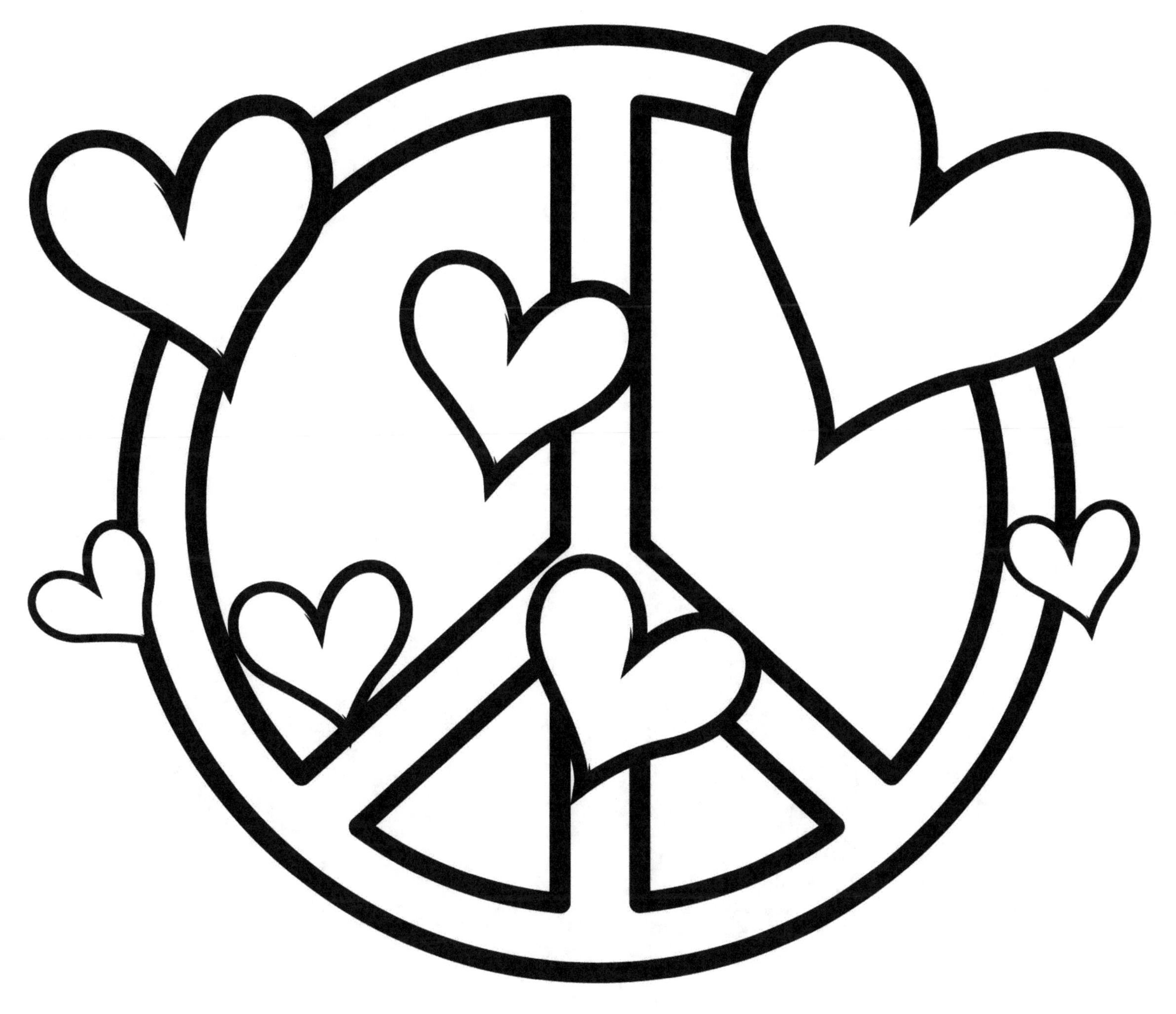

MUSIC
PEACE
LOVE

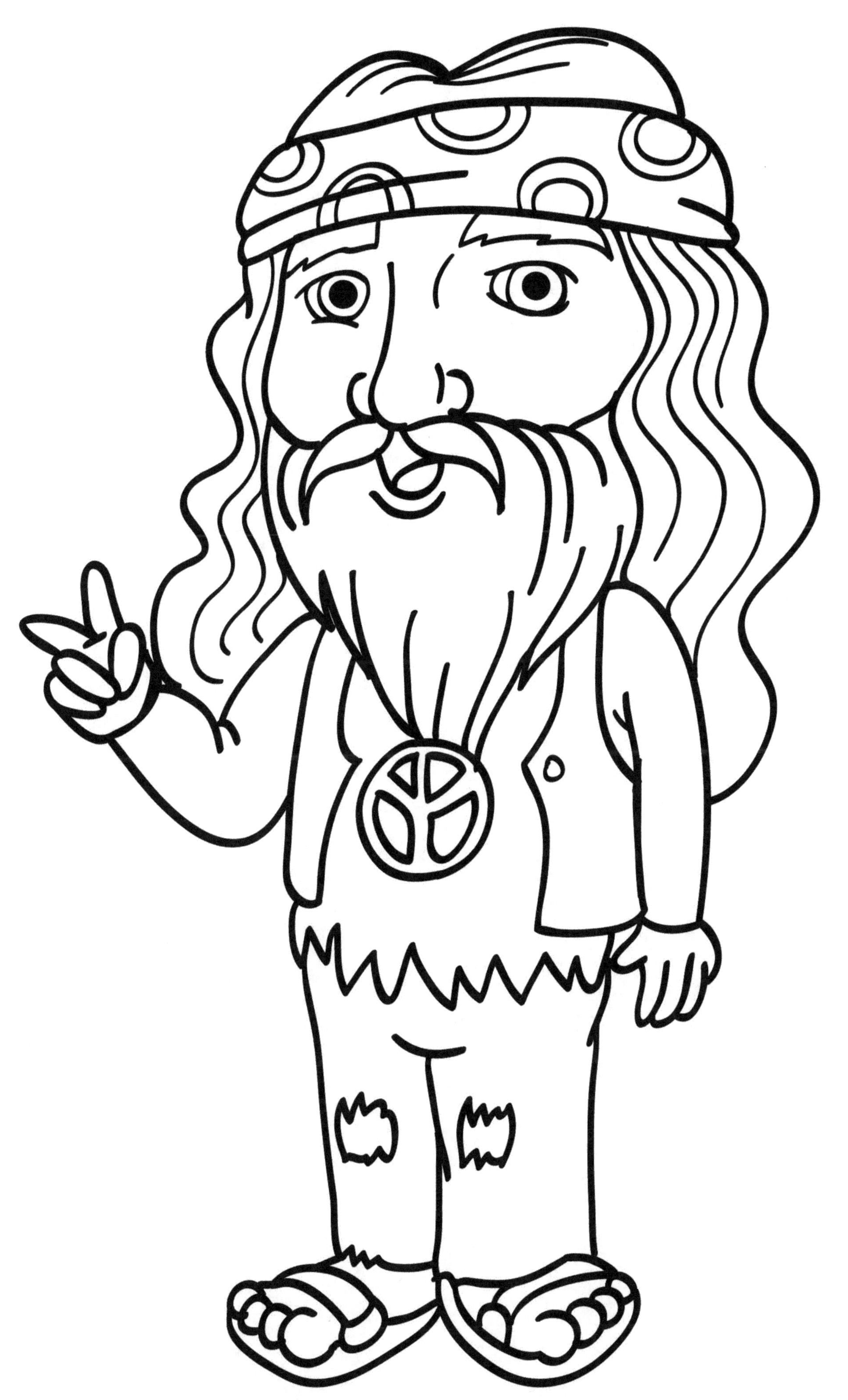

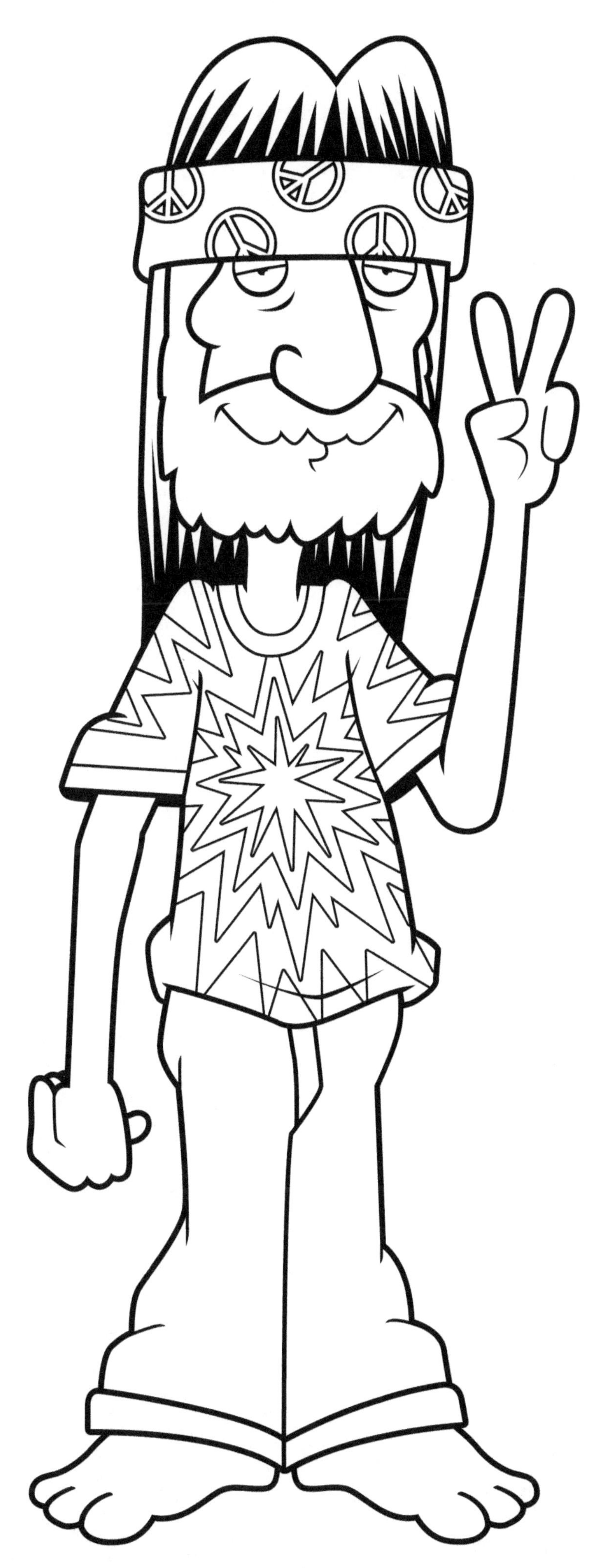

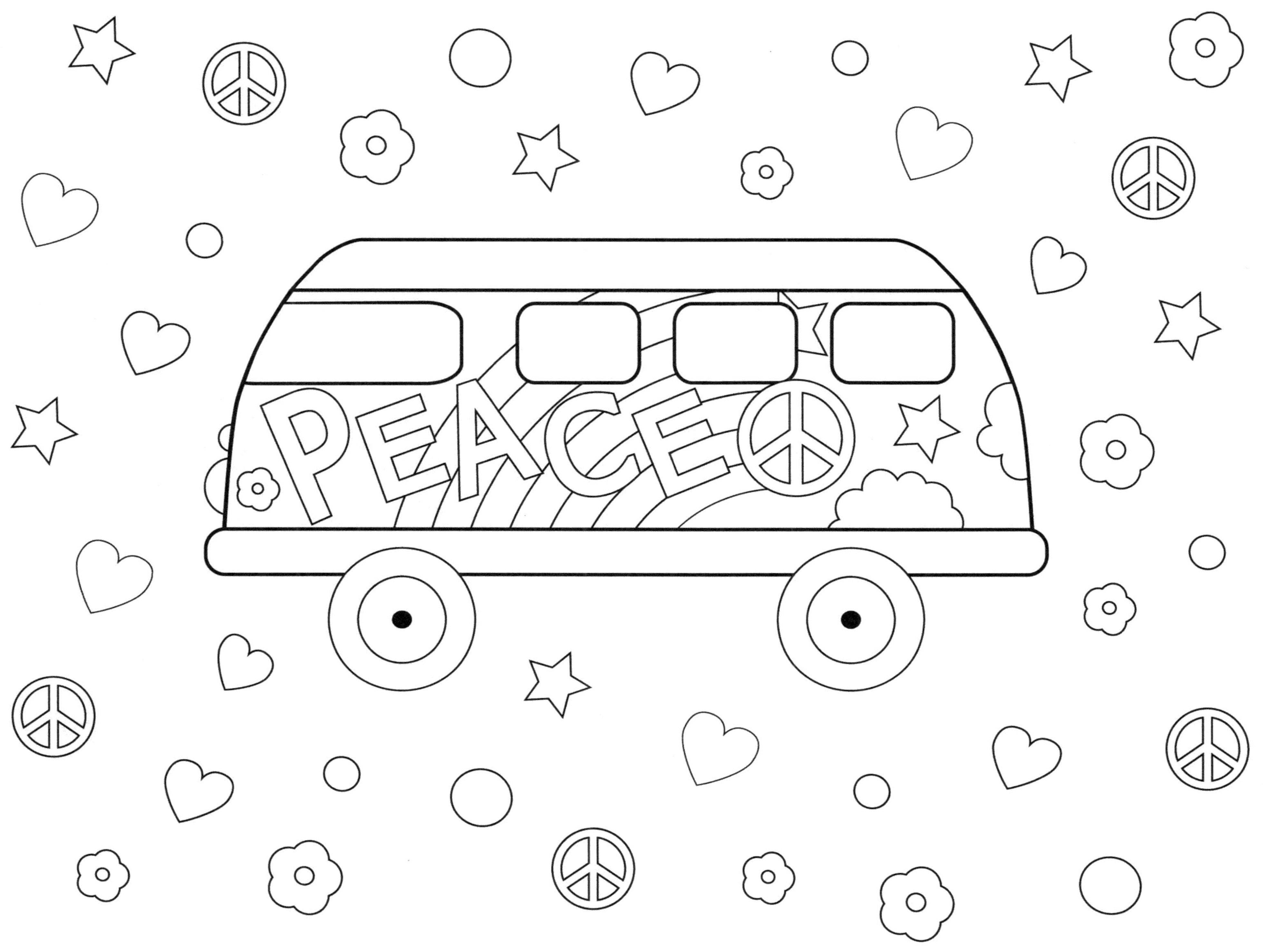
PEACE

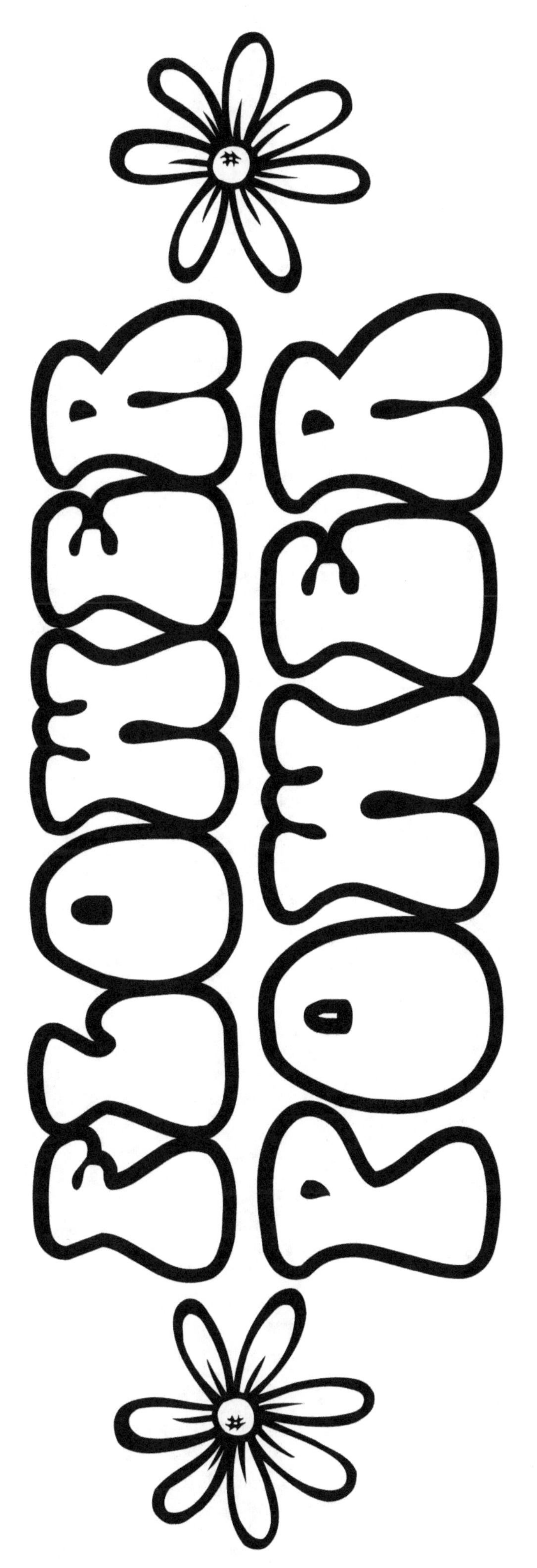
FLOWER
POWER

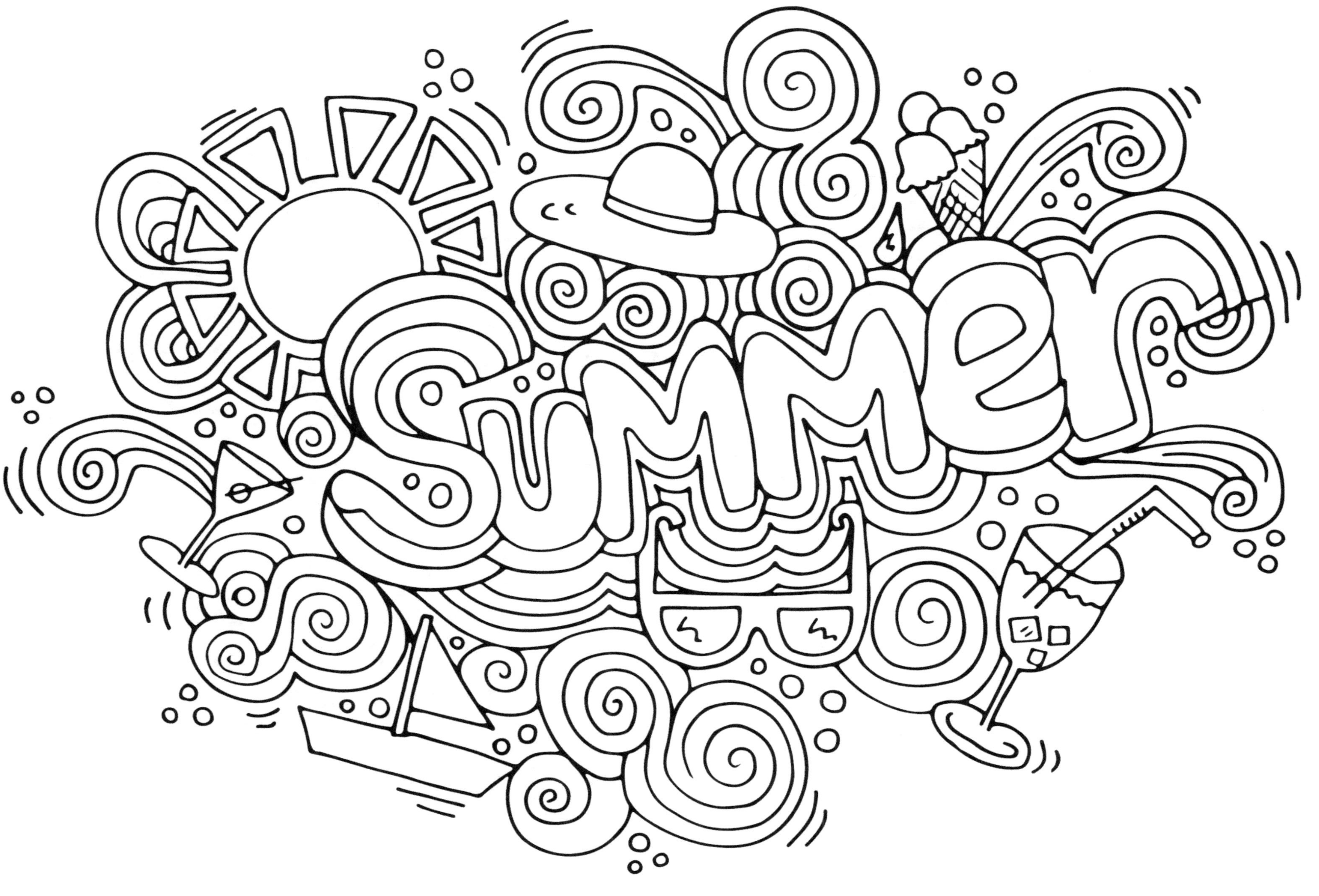
Summer

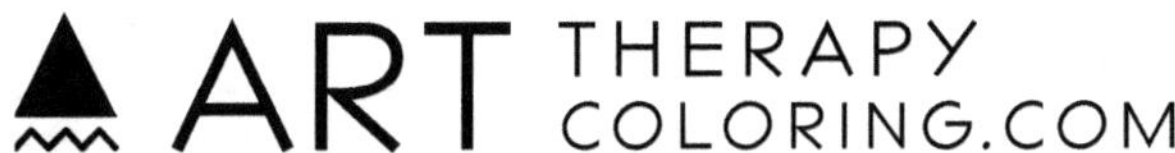

Test Your Colors

Drawings

Drawings

Drawings

More By ART THERAPY COLORING.COM

Best Selling Art Therapy Coloring Books

Coloring Books For Adults:

- Zombie Coloring Book: Black Background
- Butterfly Coloring Book For Adults: Black Background
- Tattoo Coloring Book: Black Background
- Coloring Books for Adults Relaxation: Native American Inspired Designs
- Fishing Coloring Book for Adults: Black Background

Coloring Books For Men:

- Coloring Book for Men: Anti-Stress Designs Vol 1
- Coloring Book For Men: Fishing Designs
- Coloring Book For Men: Tattoo Designs
- Coloring Books for Men: Hunting
- Coloring Book For Men: Biker Designs

Coloring Books For Seniors:

- Coloring Book For Seniors: Nature Designs Vol 1
- Coloring Book For Seniors: Anti-Stress Designs Vol 1
- Coloring Books for Seniors: Relaxing Designs
- Coloring Book For Seniors: Floral Designs Vol 1
- Coloring Book For Seniors: Ocean Designs Vol 1

Coloring Books For Teens and Tweens:

- Coloring Books For Teens: Ocean Designs
- Coloring Books for Teen Girls Vol 1
- Teen Inspirational Coloring Books
- Coloring Book for Teens: Anti-Stress Designs Vol 1
- Tween Coloring Books For Girls: Cute Animals

Coloring Books For Older Kids:

- Coloring Books For Girls: Cute Animals
- Horse Coloring Book For Girls
- Coloring Books For Boys: Sharks
- Coloring Books for Boys: Animal Designs
- Unicorn Coloring Book for Girls
- Detailed Coloring Books For Kids

Art Therapy Coloring Books

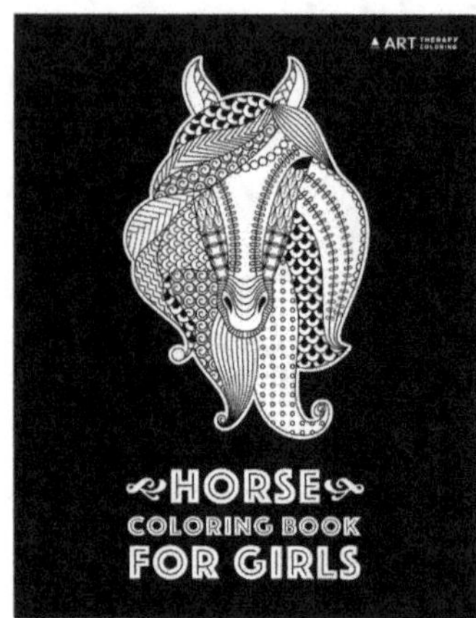

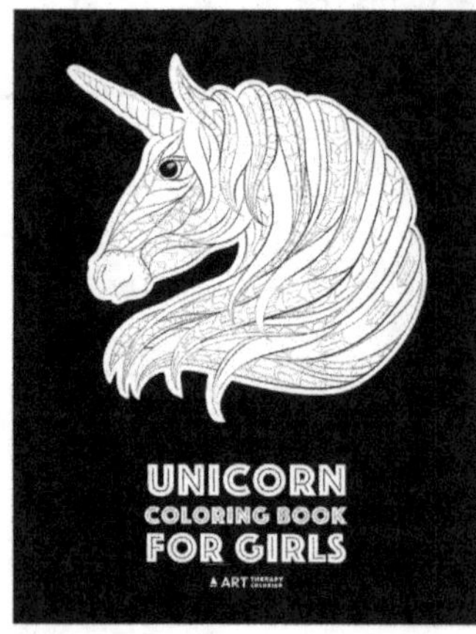

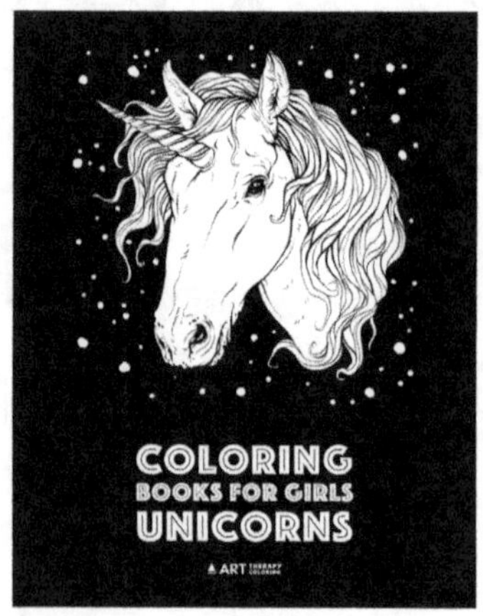

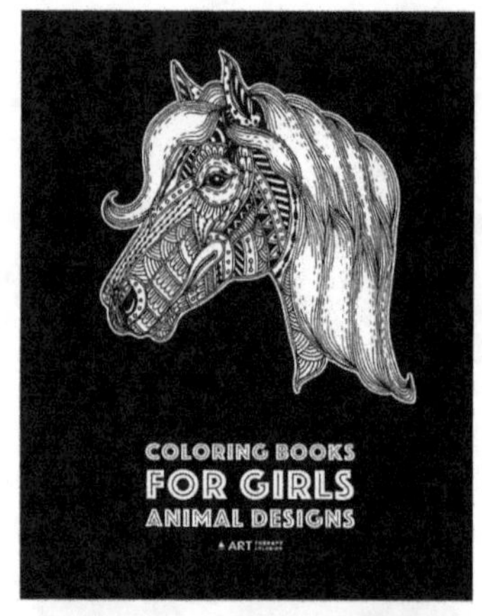

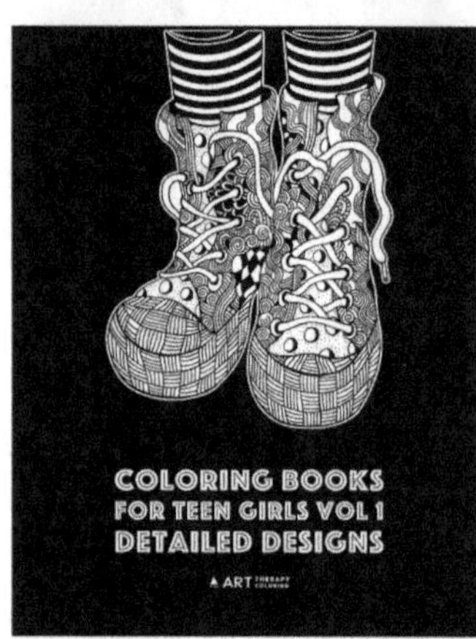

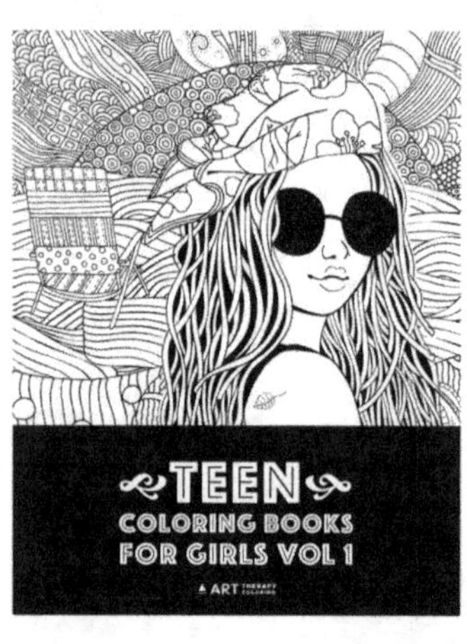

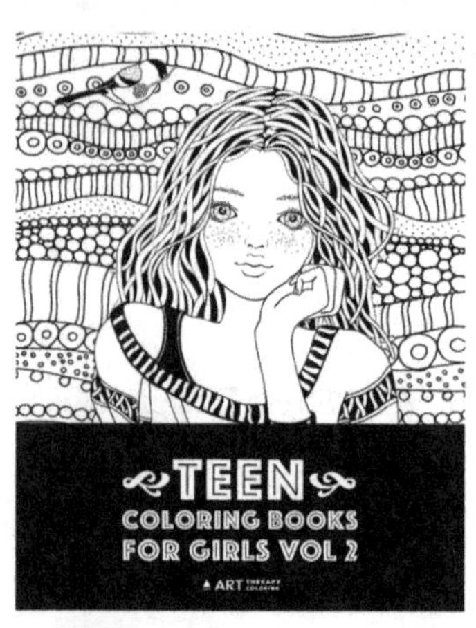

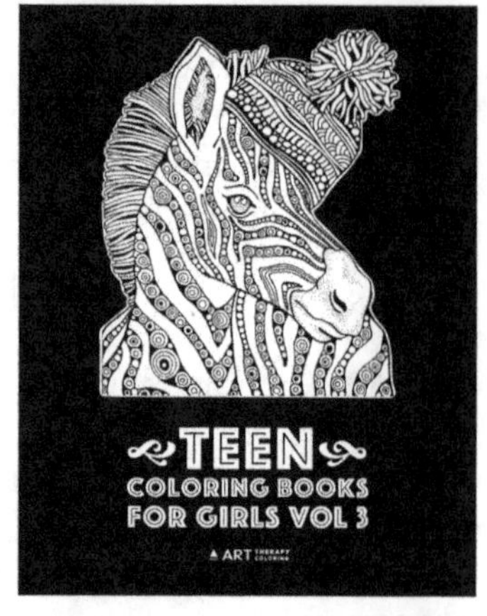

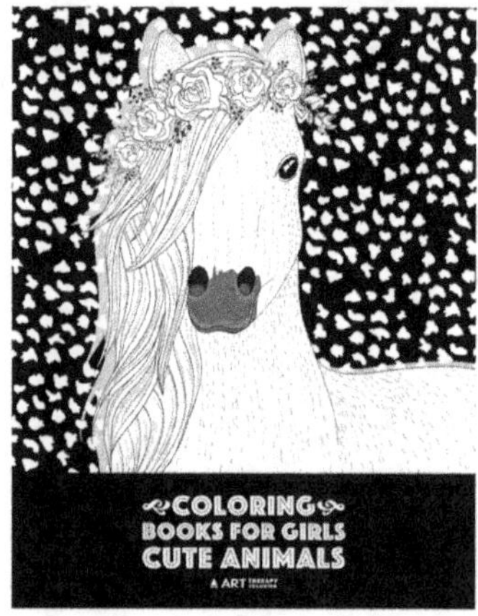

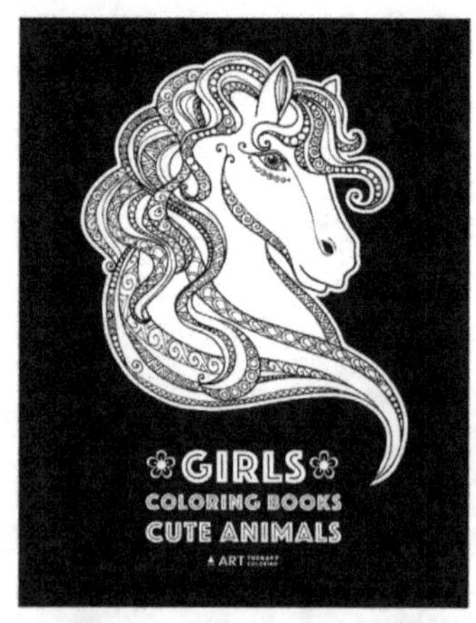

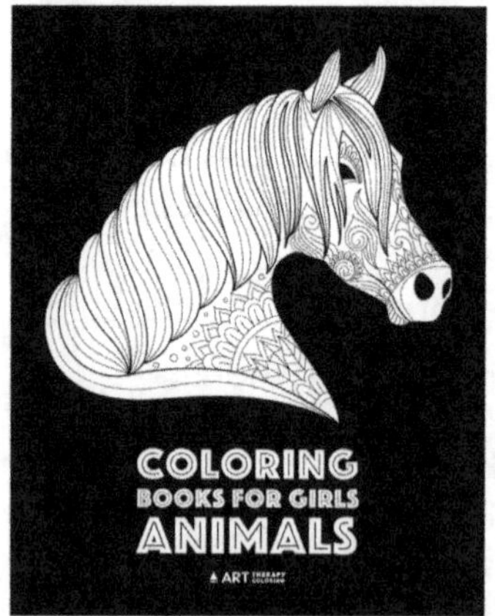

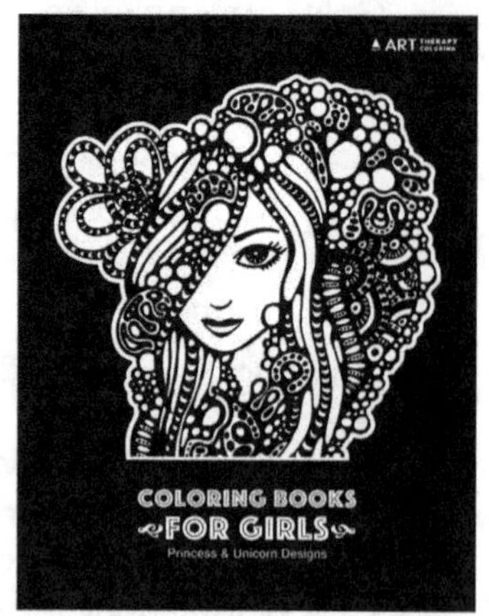

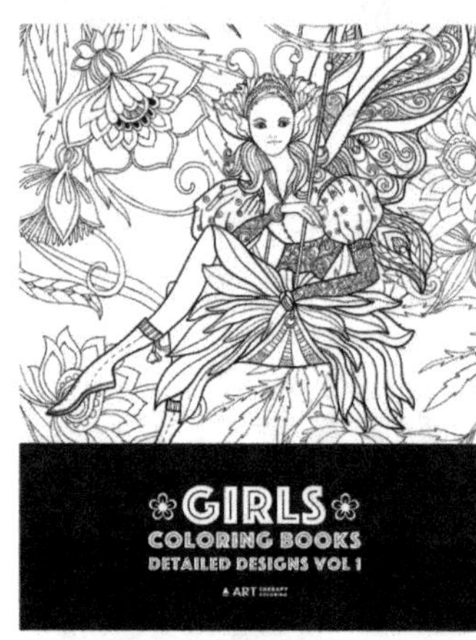

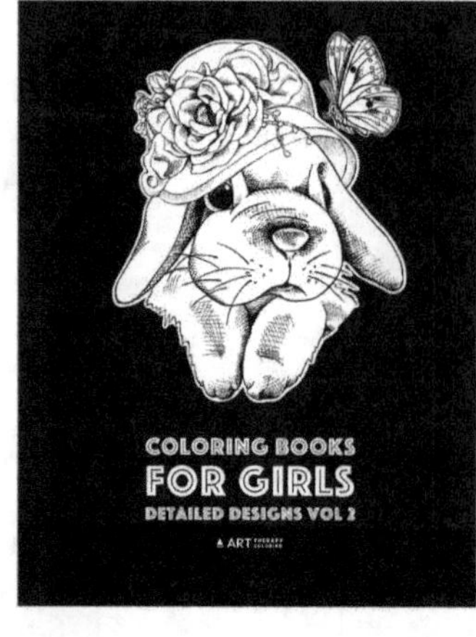

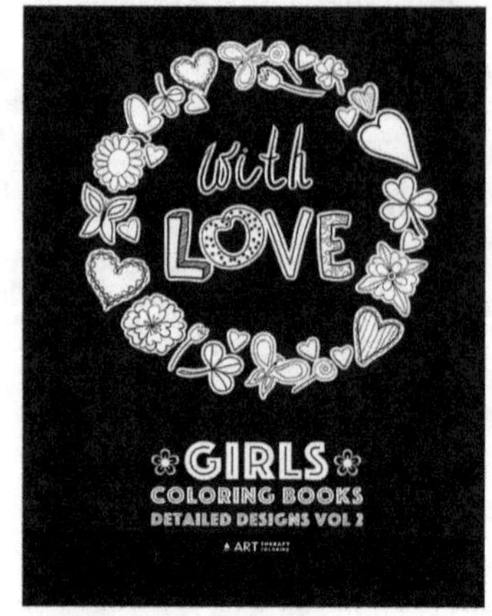

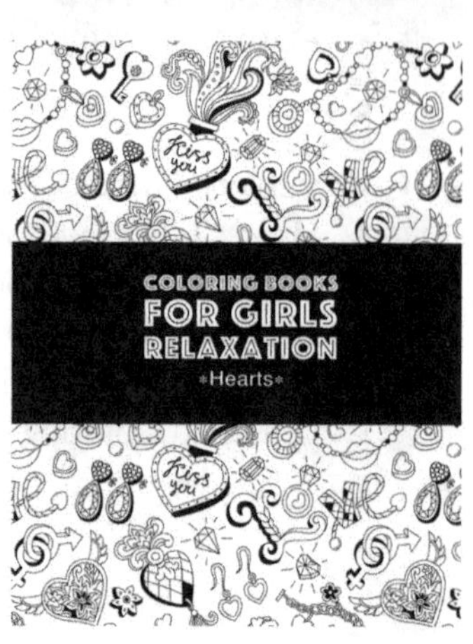

Art Therapy Coloring Books

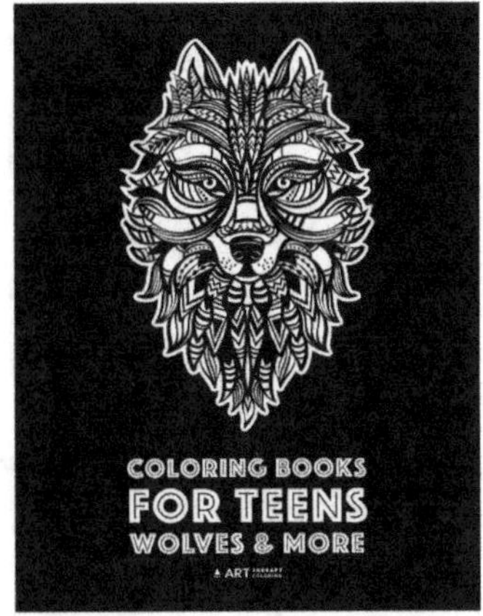

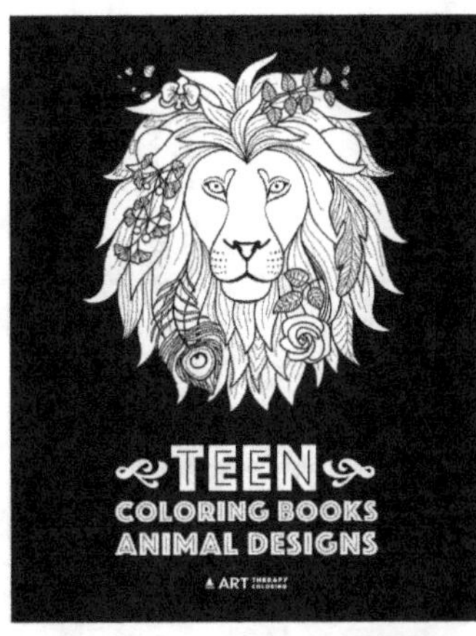

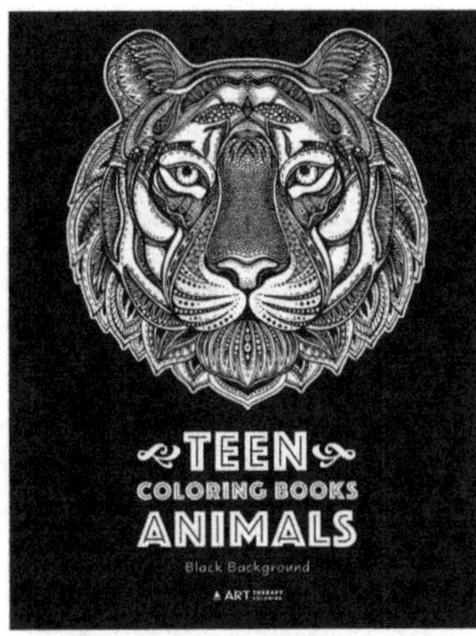

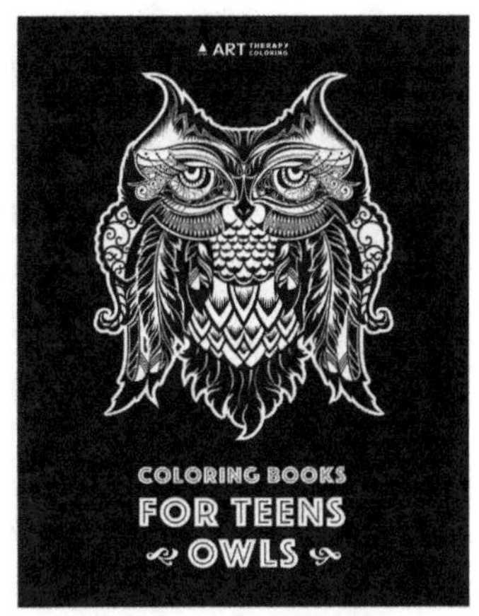

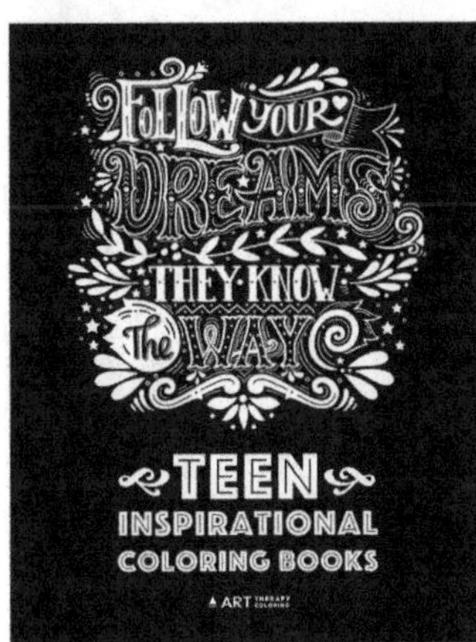

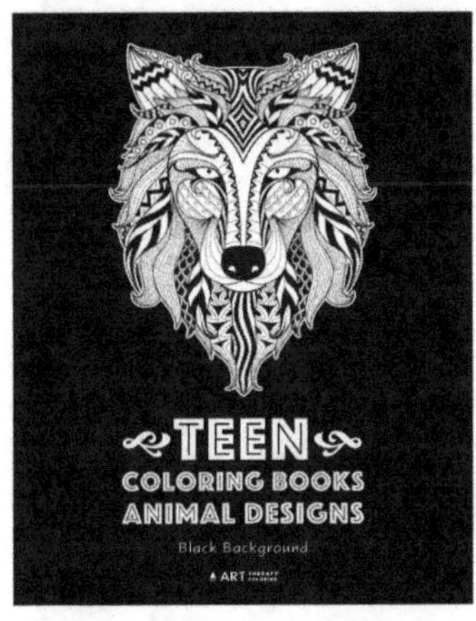

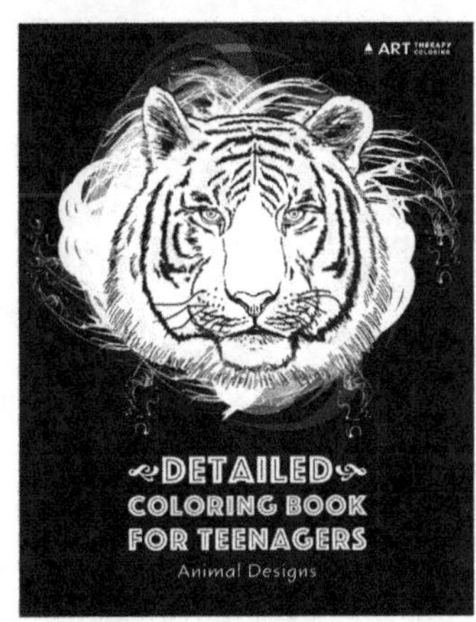

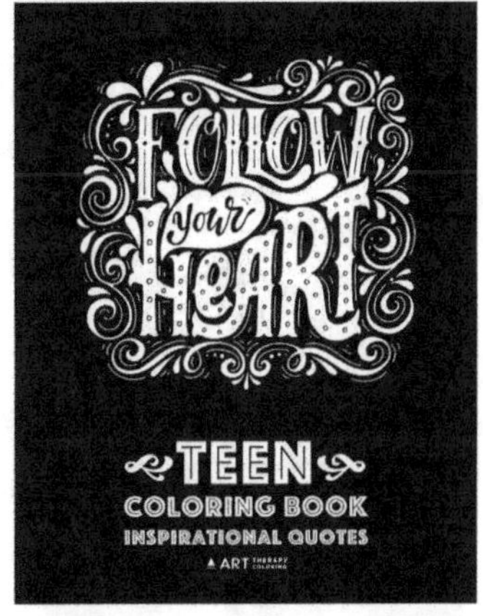

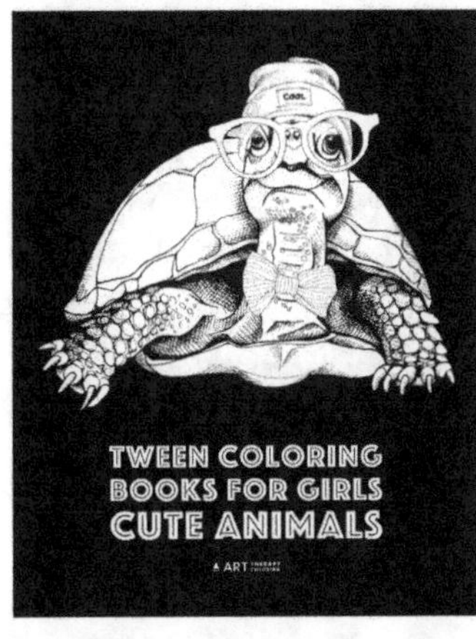

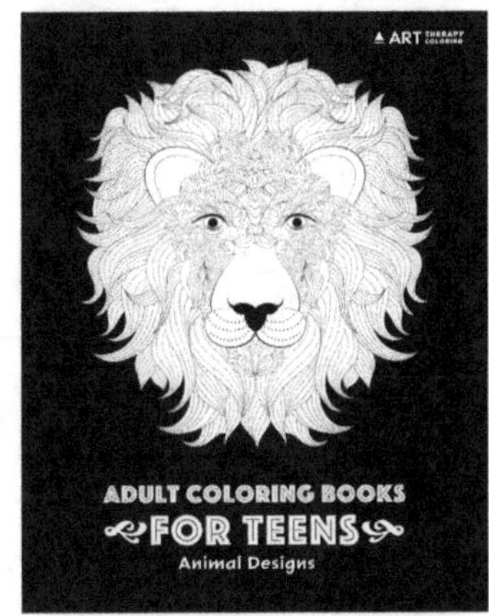

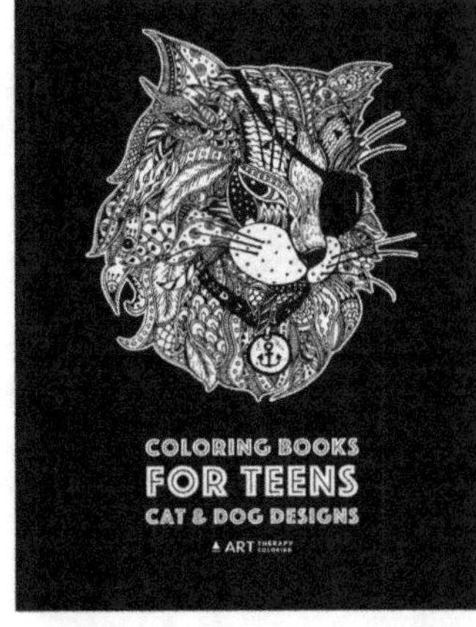

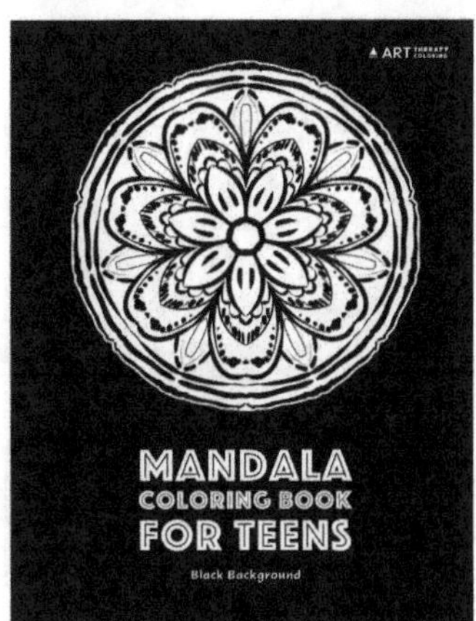

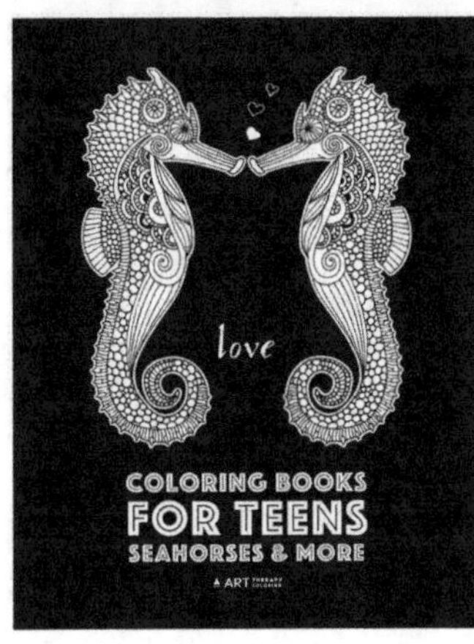

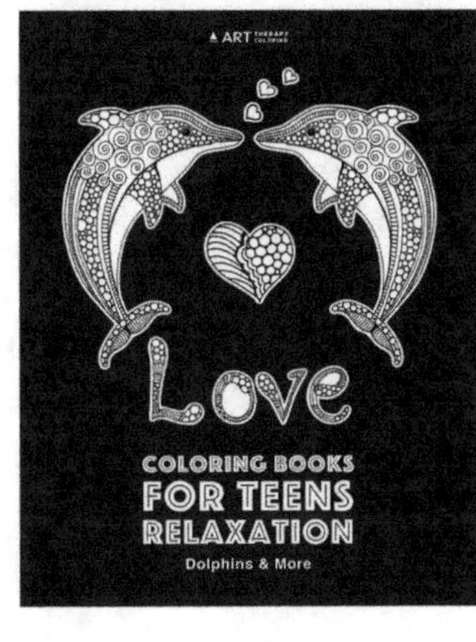

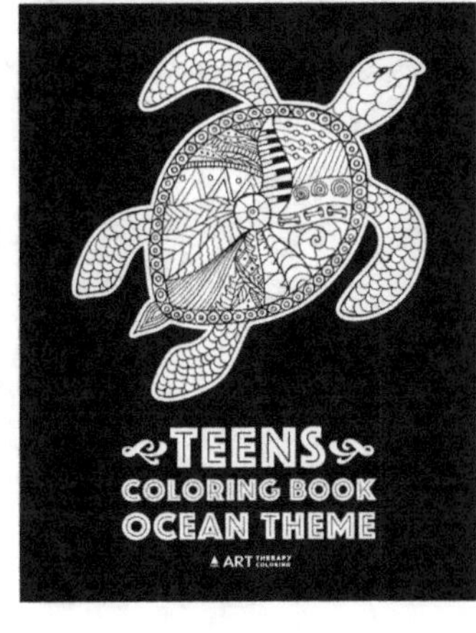

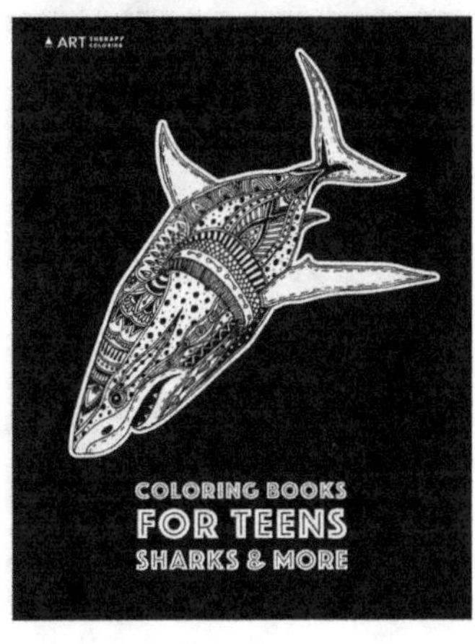

Art Therapy Coloring Books

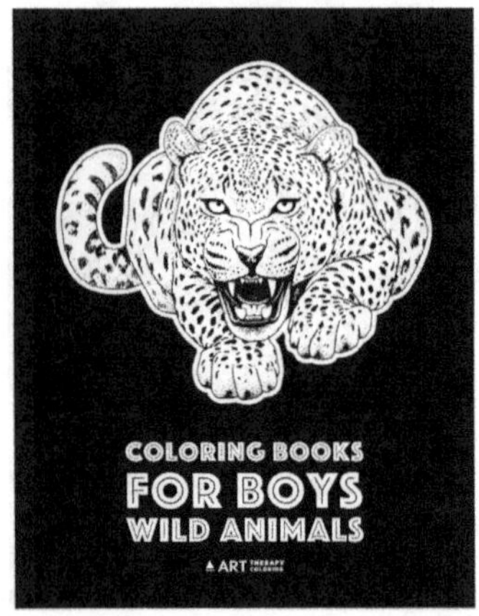

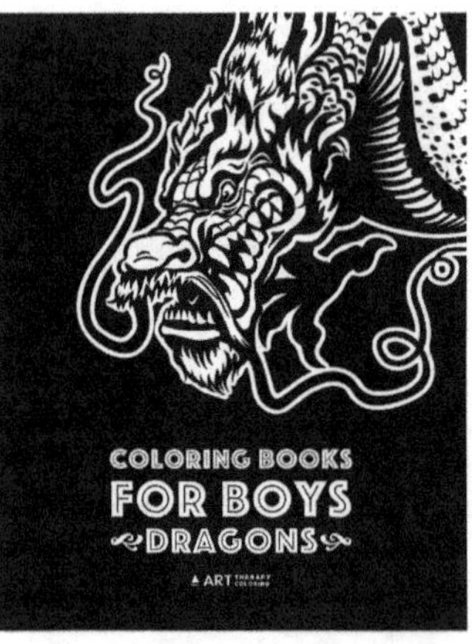

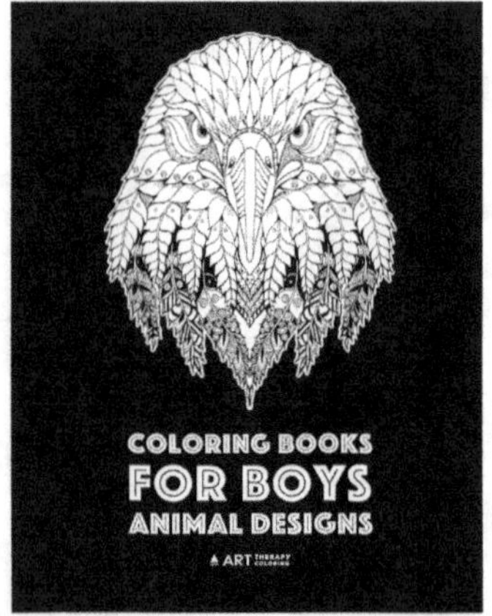

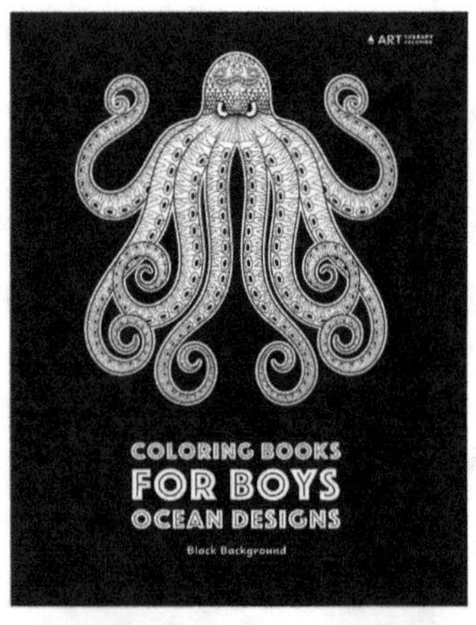

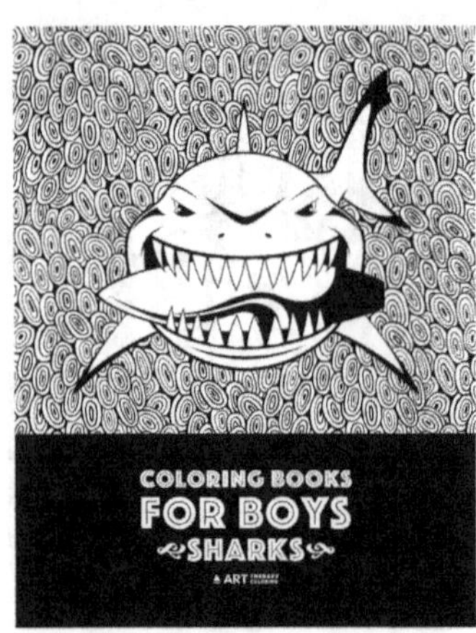

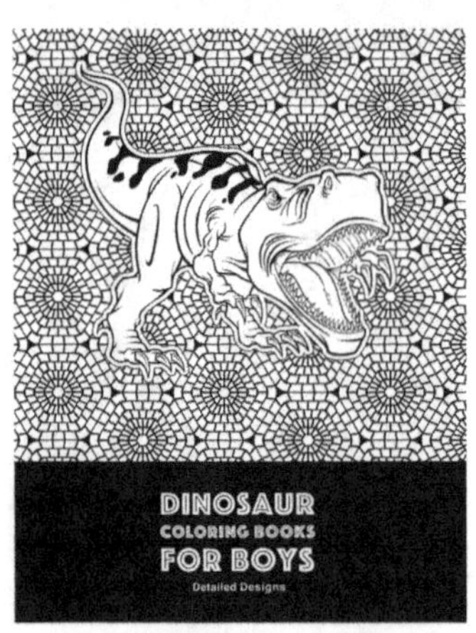

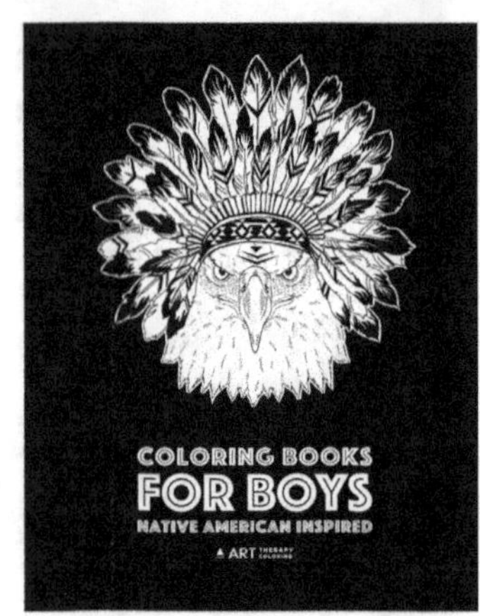

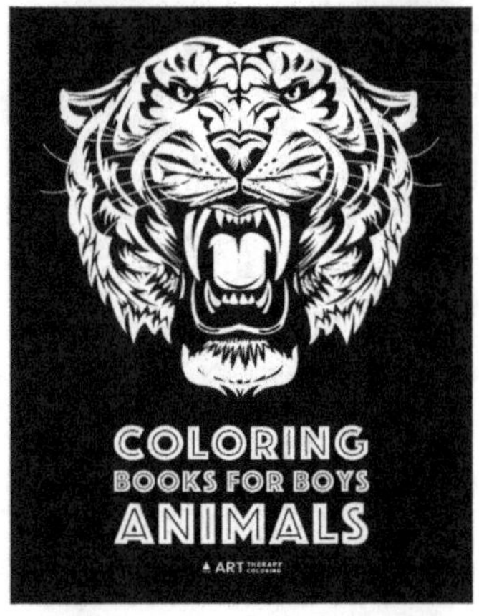

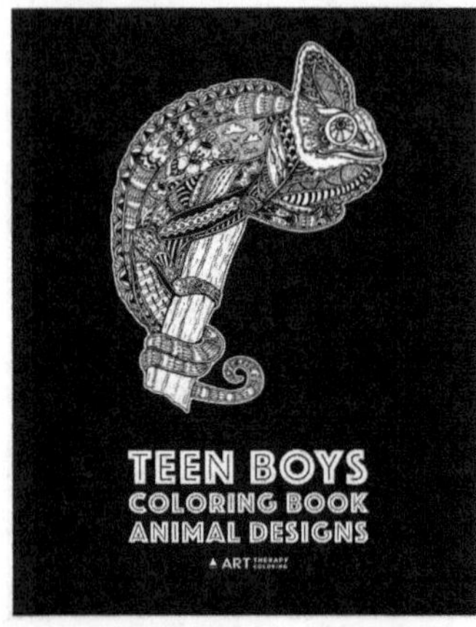

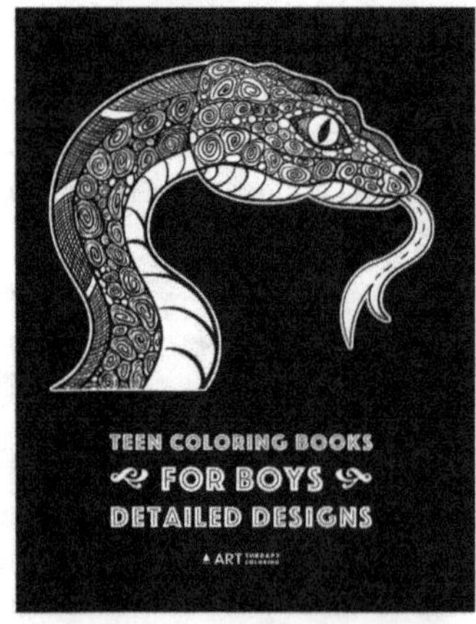

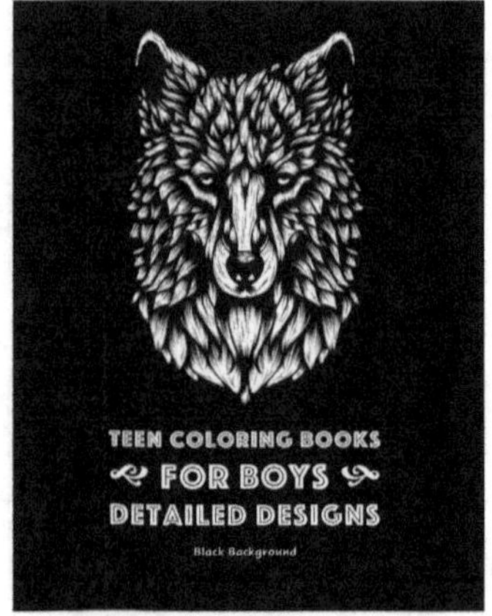

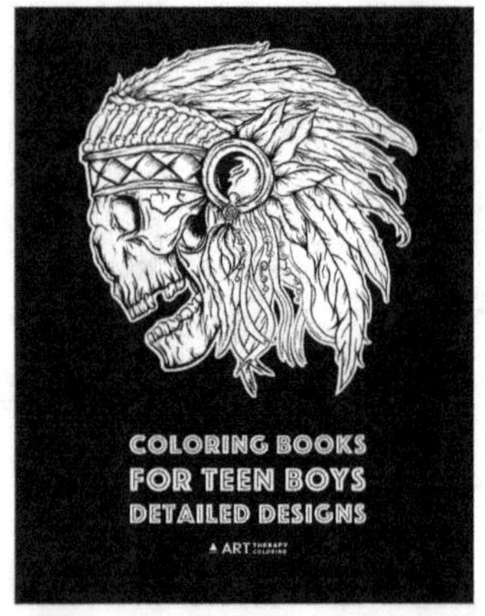

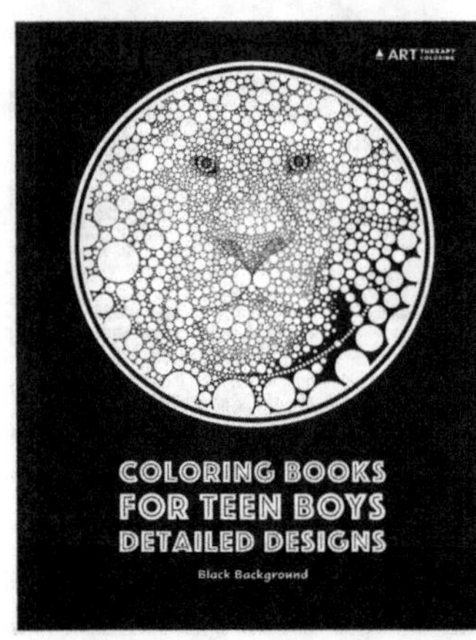

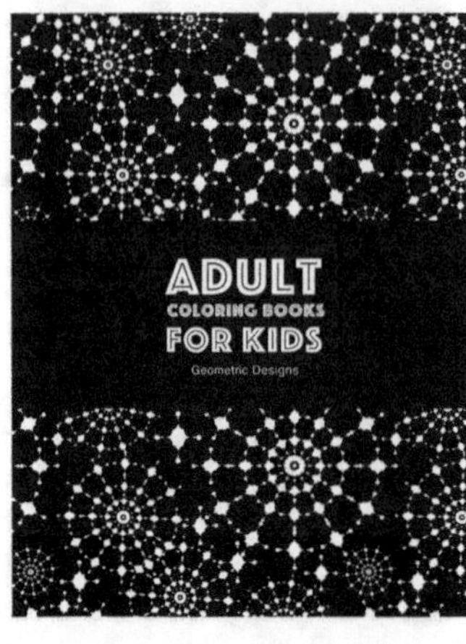

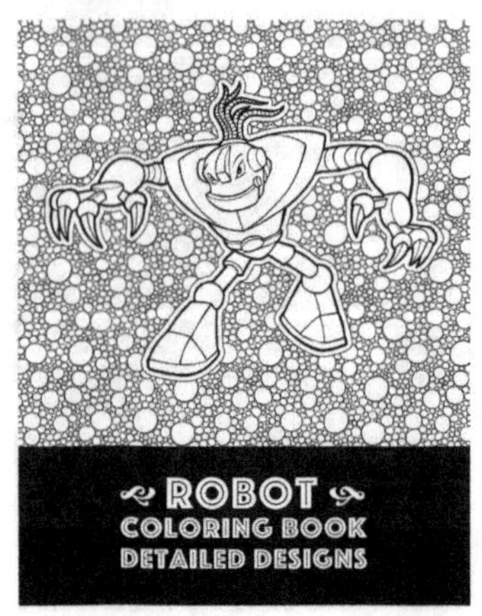

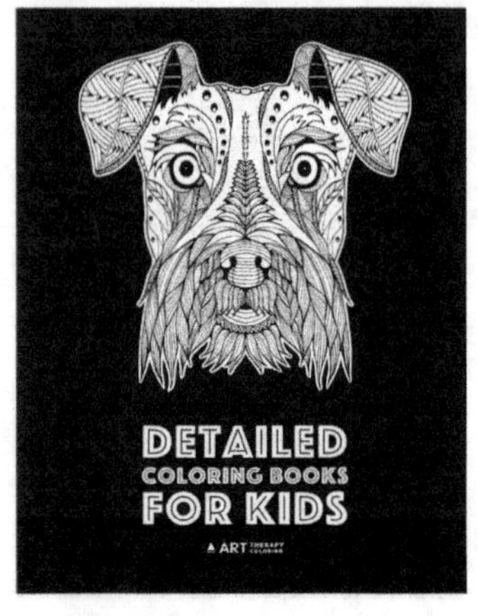

Art Therapy Coloring Books

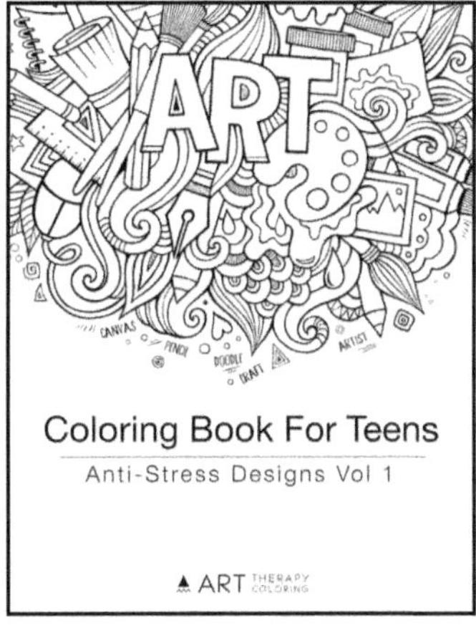

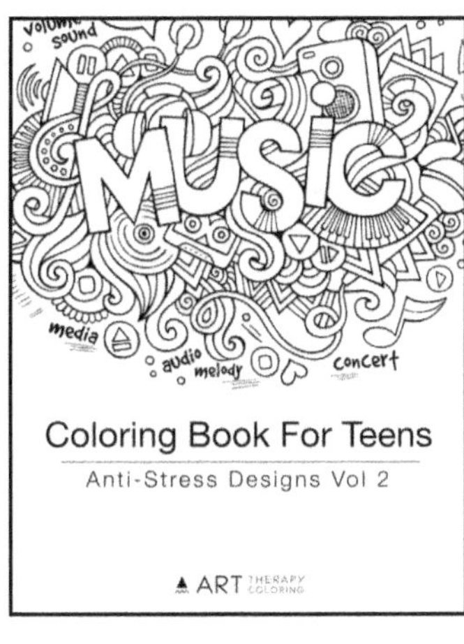

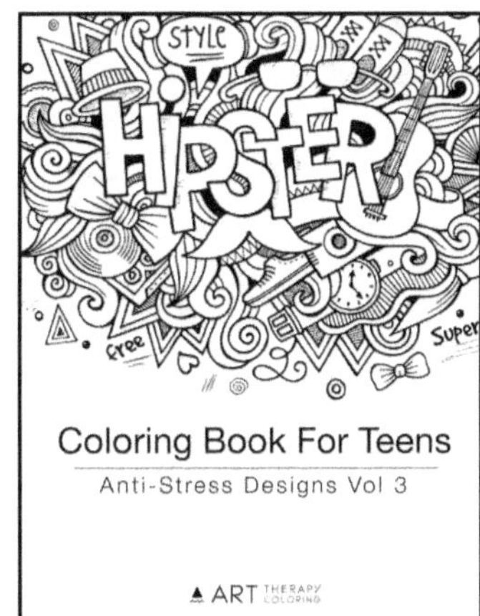

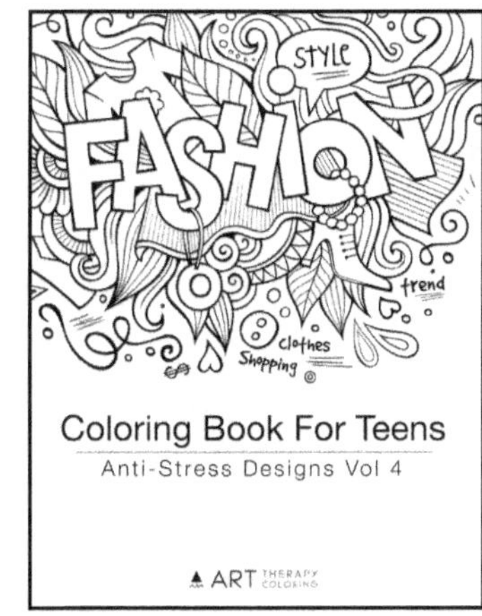

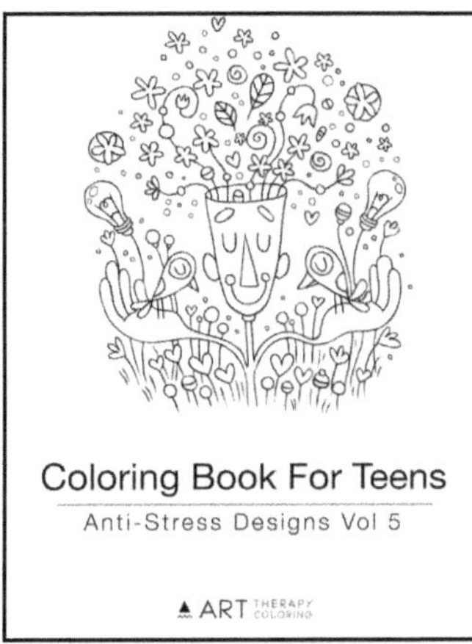

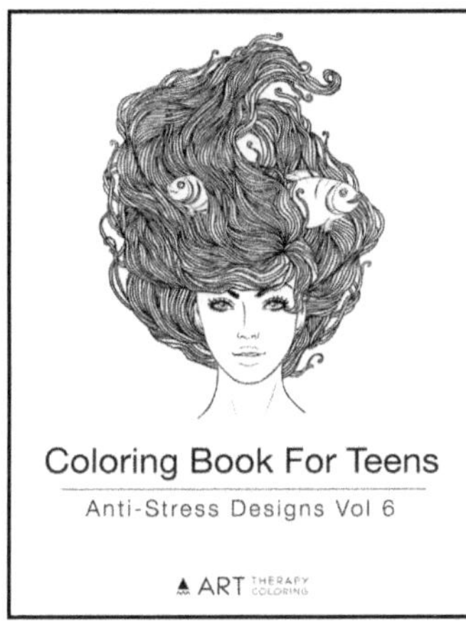

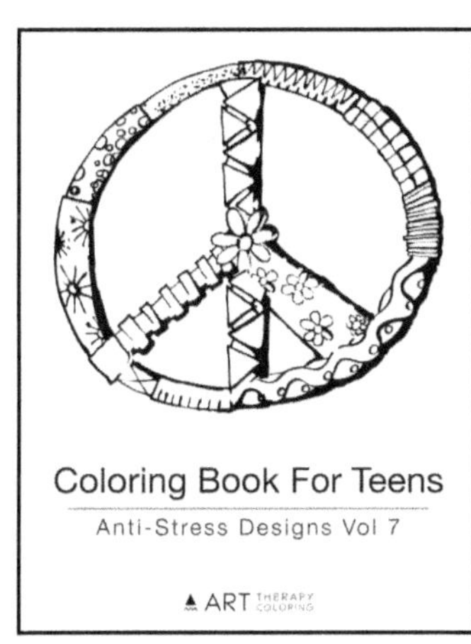

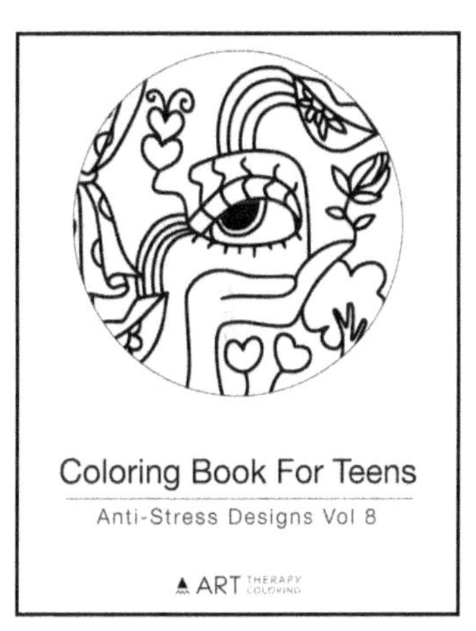

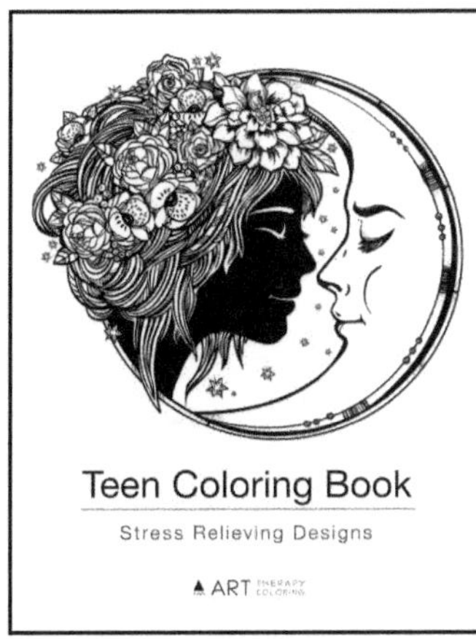

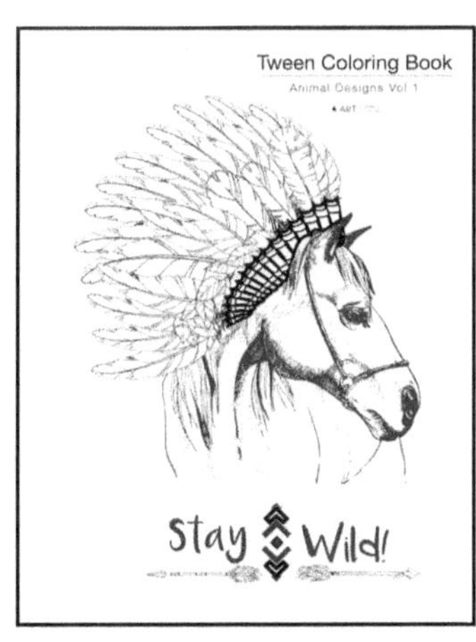

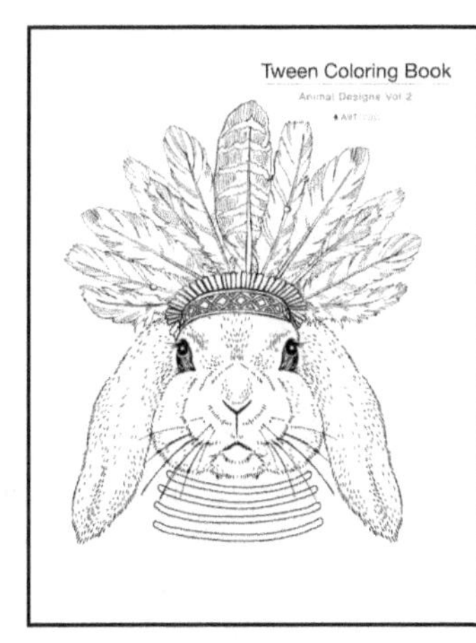

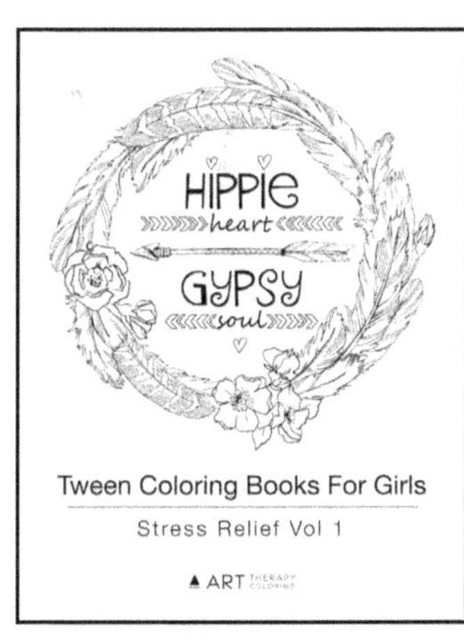

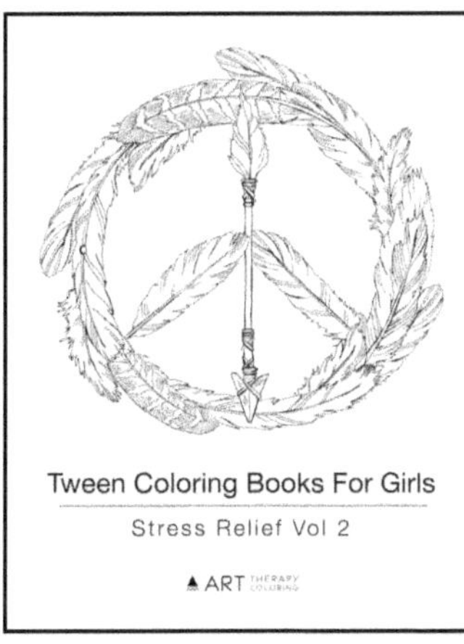

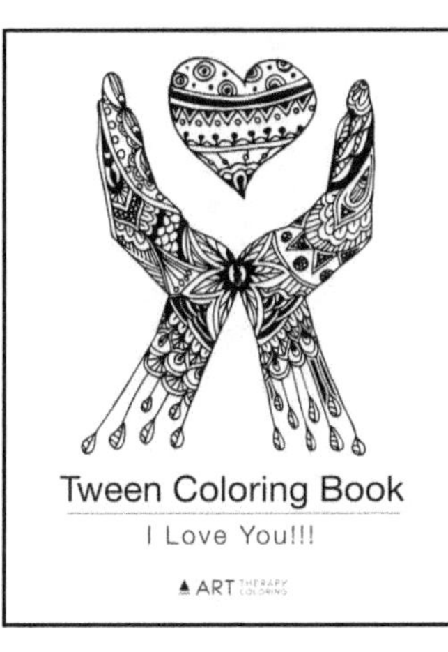

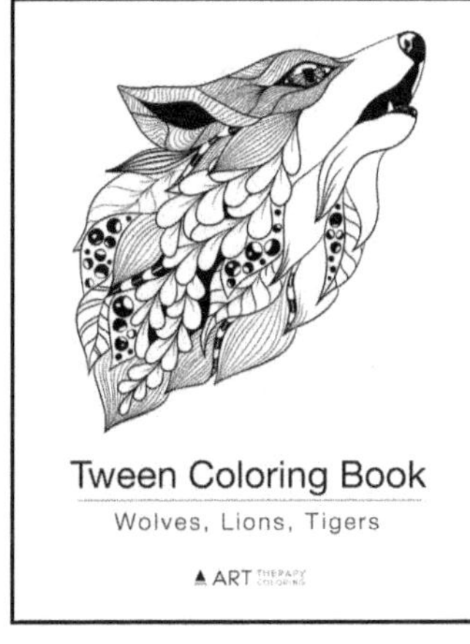

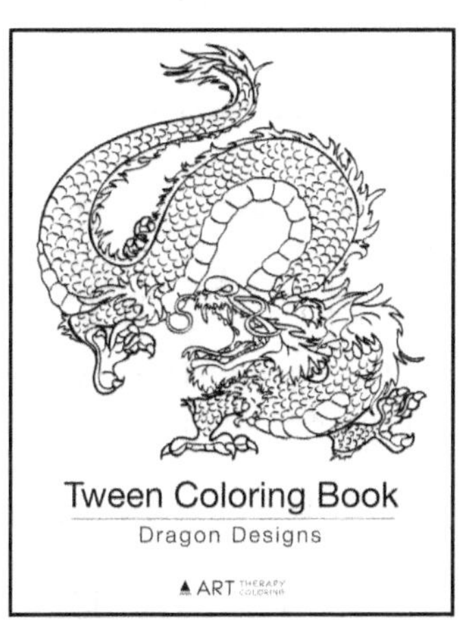

Coloring Book For Teens
Anti-Stress Designs Vol 7

Published by:
Art Therapy Coloring
www.arttherapycoloring.com

ISBN: 978-1-944427-22-1

www.ingramcontent.com/pod-product-compliance
Lightning Source LLC
LaVergne TN
LVHW080336110826
845155LV00027B/249
* 9 7 8 1 9 4 4 4 2 7 2 2 1 *